The Chocolate War

and Related Readings

McDougal Littell
A HOUGHTON MIFFLIN COMPANY
Evanston, Illinois • Boston • Dallas

Acknowledgments

Alfred A. Knopf, Inc.: *The Chocolate War* by Robert Cormier. Copyright © 1974 by Robert Cormier. Reprinted by arrangement with Alfred A. Knopf, Inc.

Brandt & Brandt Literary Agents, Inc.: "Some Opposites of Good," from *The Girl from Cardigan* by Leslie Norris, published by Gibbs M. Smith, Inc. Copyright © 1988 by Leslie Norris. Reprinted by permission of Brandt & Brandt Literary Agents, Inc.

Harcourt Brace & Company: Excerpts from *Crews: Gang Members Talk to Maria Hinojosa* by Maria Hinojosa. Copyright © 1995 by Maria Hinojosa. Reprinted by permission of the publisher.

Philip Cioffari: "Breaking Bones" by Philip Cioffari in *The Worcester Review*, Volume 11, No. 1, 1989. Reprinted by permission of the author.

Scribner and Jonathan Cape: "White Places," from *Bad Girls* by Mary Flanagan. Copyright © 1984 by Mary Flanagan. Reprinted with permission from Scribner, a division of Simon & Schuster, and from Jonathan Cape.

Writers House, Inc.: Excerpt from "Bad Company" by Rebecca Barry in *Seventeen* magazine, September 1995. Copyright © 1994 by Rebecca Barry. Reprinted by permission of Writers House, Inc., on behalf of the author.

Cover illustration Copyright © 1997 John Howard.
Author image: AP/Wide World.

2004 Impression.

Printed in the United States of America.

ISBN 0-395-87479-3

8 9 10 11 12 13 14 15 16 17 18 – DCI – 09 08 07 06 05 04

Contents

The Chocolate War

Robert Cormier

This one's for my son, Peter.
With love.

Chapter 1

They murdered him.

As he turned to take the ball, a dam burst against the side of his head and a hand grenade shattered his stomach. Engulfed by nausea, he pitched toward the grass. His mouth encountered gravel, and he spat frantically, afraid that some of his teeth had been knocked out. Rising to his feet, he saw the field through drifting gauze but held on until everything settled into place, like a lens focusing, making the world sharp again, with edges.

The second play called for a pass. Fading back, he picked up a decent block and cocked his arm, searching for a receiver—maybe the tall kid they called The Goober. Suddenly, he was caught from behind and whirled violently, a toy boat caught in a whirlpool. Landing on his knees, hugging the ball, he urged himself to ignore the pain that gripped his groin, knowing that it was important to betray no sign of distress, remembering The Goober's advice, "Coach is testing you, testing, and he's looking for guts."

I've got guts, Jerry murmured, getting up by degrees, careful not to displace any of his bones or sinews. A telephone rang in his ears. Hello, hello, I'm still here. When he moved his lips, he tasted the acid of dirt and grass and gravel. He was aware of the other players around him, helmeted and grotesque, creatures from an unknown world. He had never felt so lonely in his life, abandoned, defenseless.

On the third play, he was hit simultaneously by

three of them: one, his knees; another, his stomach; a third, his head—the helmet no protection at all. His body seemed to telescope into itself but all the parts didn't fit, and he was stunned by the knowledge that pain isn't just one thing—it is cunning and various, sharp here and sickening there, burning here and clawing there. He clutched himself as he hit the ground. The ball squirted away. His breath went away, like the ball—a terrible stillness pervaded him—and then, at the onset of panic, his breath came back again. His lips sprayed wetness and he was grateful for the sweet cool air that filled his lungs. But when he tried to get up, his body mutinied against movement. He decided the hell with it. He'd go to sleep right here, right out on the fifty yard line, the hell with trying out for the team, screw everything, he was going to sleep, he didn't care anymore . . .

"Renault!"

Ridiculous, someone calling his name.

"Renault!"

The coach's voice scraped like sandpaper against his ears. He opened his eyes flutteringly. "I'm all right," he said to nobody in particular, or to his father maybe. Or the coach. He was unwilling to abandon this lovely lassitude but he had to, of course. He was sorry to leave the earth, and he was vaguely curious about how he was going to get up, with both legs smashed and his skull battered in. He was astonished to find himself on his feet, intact, bobbing like one of those toy novelties dangling from car windows, but erect.

"For Christ's sake," the coach bellowed, his voice juicy with contempt. A spurt of saliva hit Jerry's cheek.

Hey, coach, you spit on me, Jerry protested. Stop the spitting, coach. What he said aloud was, "I'm all right, coach," because he was a coward about stuff like that, thinking one thing and saying another, planning one thing and doing another—he had been Peter a thousand times and a thousand cocks had crowed in his lifetime.

"How tall are you, Renault?"

"Five nine," he gasped, still fighting for breath.

"Weight?"

"One forty-five," he said, looking the coach straight in the eye.

"Soaking wet, I'll bet," the coach said sourly. "What the hell you want to play football for? You need more meat on those bones. What the hell you trying to play quarterback for? You'd make a better end. Maybe."

The coach looked like an old gangster: broken nose, a scar on his cheek like a stitched shoestring. He needed a shave, his stubble like slivers of ice. He growled and swore and was merciless. But a helluva coach, they said. The coach stared at him now, the dark eyes probing, pondering. Jerry hung in there, trying not to sway, trying not to faint.

"All right," the coach said in disgust. "Show up tomorrow. Three o'clock sharp or you're through before you start."

Inhaling the sweet sharp apple air through his nostrils—he was afraid to open his mouth wide, wary of any movement that was not absolutely essential—he walked tentatively toward the sidelines, listening to the coach barking at the other guys. Suddenly, he loved that voice, "Show up tomorrow."

He trudged away from the field, blinking against the afternoon sun, toward the locker room at the gym. His knees were liquid and his body light as air, suddenly.

Know what? he asked himself, a game he played sometimes.

What?

I'm going to make the team.

Dreamer, dreamer.

Not a dream: it's the truth.

As Jerry took another deep breath, a pain appeared, distant, small—a radar signal of distress. Bleep, I'm here. Pain. His feet scuffled through crazy cornflake leaves. A strange happiness invaded him. He knew he'd been massacred by the oncoming players, capsized and dumped humiliatingly on the ground. But he'd survived—he'd gotten to his feet. "You'd made a better end." Was the coach thinking he might try him at end? Any position, as long as he made the team. The bleep grew larger, localized now, between his ribs on the right side. He thought of his mother and how drugged she was at the end, not recognizing anyone, neither Jerry nor his father. The exhilaration of the moment vanished and he sought it in vain, like seeking ecstasy's memory an instant after jacking off and encountering only shame and guilt.

Nausea began to spread through his stomach, warm and oozy and evil.

"Hey," he called weakly. To nobody. Nobody there to listen.

He managed to make it back to the school. By the time he had sprawled himself on the floor of the lavatory, his head hanging over the lip of the toilet bowl and the smell of disinfectant stinging his eyeballs, the nausea had passed and the bleep of pain had faded. Sweat moved like small moist bugs on his forehead.

And then, without warning, he vomited.

Chapter 2

Obie was bored. Worse than bored. He was disgusted. He was also tired. It seemed he was always tired these days. He went to bed tired and he woke up tired. He found himself yawning constantly. Most of all, he was tired of Archie. Archie the bastard. The bastard that Obie alternately hated and admired. For instance, at this minute he hated Archie with a special burning hate that was part of the boredom and the weariness. Notebook in hand, pencil poised, Obie looked at Archie now with fierce anger, furious at the way Archie sat there in the bleachers, his blond hair tossing lightly in the breeze, enjoying himself, for crying out loud, even though he knew that Obie would be late for work and yet keeping him here, stalling, killing time.

"You're a real bastard," Obie said finally, his frustration erupting, like a coke exploding from a bottle after you shake it. "You know that?"

Archie turned and smiled at him benevolently, like a goddam king passing out favors.

"Jesus," Obie said, exasperated.

"Don't swear, Obie," Archie chided. "You'll have to tell it in confession."

"Look who's talking. I don't know how you had the nerve to receive communion at chapel this morning."

"It doesn't take nerve, Obie. When you march down to the rail, you're receiving The Body, man. Me, I'm just chewing a wafer they buy by the pound in Worcester."

Obie looked away in disgust.

"And when you say 'Jesus,' you're talking about your leader. But when I say 'Jesus,' I'm talking about a guy who walked the earth for thirty-three years like any other guy but caught the imagination of some *PR* cats. *PR* for Public Relations, in case you don't know, Obie."

Obie didn't bother to answer. You couldn't ever win an argument with Archie. He was too quick with the words. Especially when he fell into one of his phony hip moods. Saying *man* and *cat,* like he was a swinger, cool, instead of a senior in a lousy little high school like Trinity.

"Come on, Archie, it's getting late," Obie said, trying to appeal to Archie's better nature. "I'm going to get fired one of these days."

"Don't whine, Obie. Besides, you hate the job. You have a subconscious wish to be fired. Then you wouldn't have to stock the shelves any more or take crap from customers or work late Saturday night instead of going to the—what is it you go to?—the Teen-Age Canteen to drool over all those broads."

Archie was uncanny. How did he know Obie hated the stupid job? How did he know that Obie hated especially those Saturday nights stalking the super-market canyons while everybody else was at the canteen?

"See? I'm doing you a favor. Enough of these late afternoons and the boss'll say, 'You're all done, Obie baby. Set free.' And you'll have one, right in front of him."

"And where'll my money come from?" Obie asked.

Archie waved his hand, signaling that he was tired of the conversation. You could see him physically withdraw although he was only a foot or two away from Obie on the bleacher bench. The shouts of the fellows from the football field below echoed feebly in the air. Archie's lower lip dropped. That meant he was concentrating. Thinking. Obie waited in anticipation, hating the thing in him that made him look at Archie in admiration. The way Archie could turn people on. Or off. The way he could dazzle you with his brilliance—those Vigil assignments that had made him practically a legend at Trinity—and the way he could disgust you with his cruelties, those strange offbeat cruelties of his, that had nothing to do with pain or violence but were somehow even worse. It made Obie uncomfortable to think of that stuff and he shrugged the thoughts away, waiting for Archie to talk, to say the name.

"Stanton," Archie said finally, whispering the name, caressing the syllables. "I think his first name is Norman."

"Right," Obie said, scrawling the name. Only two more to go. Archie had to come up with ten names by four o'clock and eight were now listed on Obie's pad.

"The assignment?" Obie prodded.

"Sidewalk."

Obie grinned as he wrote the word. Sidewalk: such an innocent word. But what Archie could do with simple things like a sidewalk and a kid like Norman Stanton whom Obie recalled as a blustering bragging character with wild red hair and eyelids matted with yellow crap.

"Hey, Obie," Archie said.

"Yeah?" Obie asked, on guard.

"You really going to be late for work? I mean—would you really lose your job?" Archie's voice was soft with concern, his eyes gentle with compassion. That's what baffled everyone about Archie—his changes of mood, the way he could be a wise bastard one minute and a great guy the next.

"I don't think they'd actually fire me. The guy who owns the place, he's a friend of the family. But I mean getting there late doesn't, like, help the cause. I'm overdue for a raise but he's holding it back until I get on the ball."

Archie nodded, all businesslike. "All right, we'll wrap it up. We'll get you on the ball. Maybe I ought to assign someone to the store, and make life interesting for your boss."

"Jeez, no," Obie said quickly. He shivered with dread, realizing how awesome Archie's power really was. Which is why you had to stay on the good side of the bastard. Buy him Hersheys all the time to satisfy his craving for chocolate. Thank God Archie didn't go in for pot or that stuff—Obie would have had to become a pusher, for crying out loud, to supply him. Obie was officially the secretary of The Vigils but he knew what the job really demanded. Carter, the president who was almost as big a bastard as Archie, said, "keep him happy, when Archie's happy, we're all happy."

"Two more names," Archie mused now. He rose and stretched. He was tall and not too heavy. He moved with a subtle rhythm, languidly, the walk of an athlete although he hated all sports and had nothing but contempt for athletes. Particularly football players and boxers, which happened to be Trinity's two major sports. Usually, Archie didn't pick athletes for assignments—he claimed they were too stupid to absorb the delicate shadings, the subtle intricacies involved. Archie disliked violence—most of his assignments were exercises in the psychological rather than the physical. That's why he got away with so much. The Trinity brothers wanted peace at any price, quiet on the campus, no broken bones. Otherwise, the sky was the limit. Which was right up Archie's alley.

"The kid they call The Goober," Archie said now.

Obie wrote down "Roland Goubert."

"Brother Eugene's room."

Obie smiled in delicious malice. He liked it when Archie involved the brothers in the assignments. Those were the most daring, of course. And someday Archie would go too far and trip himself up. In the meantime, Brother Eugene would do. He was a peaceful sort, made to order for Archie, naturally.

The sun vanished behind floating clouds. Archie brooded, isolating himself again. The wind rose, kicking puffs of dust from the football field. The field needed seeding. The bleachers also needed attention— they sagged, peeling paint like leprosy on the benches. The shadows of the goal posts sprawled on the field like grotesque crosses. Obie shivered.

"What the hell do they think I am?" Archie asked.

Obie remained silent. The question didn't seem to require an answer. It was as if Archie was talking to himself.

"These goddam assignments," Archie said. "Do they think it's easy?" His voice dripped sadness. "And the black box . . ."

Obie yawned. He was tired. And uncomfortable. He always yawned and got tired and uncomfortable when he found himself in situations like this, not knowing how to proceed, surprised at the anguish in Archie's voice. Or was Archie putting him on? You never knew about Archie. Obie was grateful when Archie finally shook his head as if warding off an evil spell.

"You're not much help, Obie."

"I never thought you needed much help, Archie."

"Don't you think I'm human, too?"

I'm not sure. That's what Obie almost said.

"All right, all right. Let's finish the damn assignments. One more name."

Obie's pencil was poised.

"Who was that kid who left the field a few minutes ago? The one they wiped out?"

"Kid named Jerry Renault. Freshman," Obie said, flipping through his notebook. He searched the *R*'s for Renault. His notebook was more complete than the school's files. It contained information, carefully coded, about everyone at Trinity, the kind of stuff that couldn't be found in official records. "Here it is. Renault, Jerome E. Son of James R. Pharmacist at Blake's. The kid's a freshman, birthday—let's see, he just turned fourteen. Oh—his mother died last spring. Cancer." There was more information about courses and records in grammar school and extracurricular activities but Obie closed the notebook as if he were lowering a coffin lid.

"Poor kid," Archie said. "Mother's dead."

Again that concern, that compassion in his voice.

Obie nodded. One more name. Who else?

"Must be hard on the poor kid."

"Right," Obie agreed, impatient.

"Know what he needs, Obie?" His voice was soft, dreamy, caressing.

"What?"

"Therapy."

The terrible word shattered the tenderness in Archie's voice.

"Therapy?"

"Right. Put him down."

"For crying out loud, Archie. You saw him out there. He's just a skinny kid trying to make the Freshman team. Coach'll grind him up like hamburger. And his mother's barely cold in the grave.

What the hell you putting him on the list for?"

"Don't let him fool you, Obie. He's a tough one. Didn't you see him get wiped out down there and still get to his feet? Tough. And stubborn. He should have stayed down on that turf, Obie. That would have been the smart thing to do. Besides, he probably needs something to keep his mind off his poor dead mother."

"You're a bastard, Archie. I said it before and I'll say it again."

"Put him down." Ice in the voice, cold as polar regions.

Obie wrote down the name. Hell, it wasn't his funeral. "Assignment?"

"I'll think of something."

"You've only got till four," Obie reminded.

"The assignment must fit the kid. That's the beauty of it, Obie."

Obie waited a minute or two and couldn't resist asking, "You running out of ideas, Archie?" The great Archie Costello running dry? The possibility was staggering to contemplate.

"Just being artistic, Obie. It's an art, you know. Take a kid like this Renault. Special circumstances." He fell silent. "Put him down for the chocolates."

Obie wrote down: *Renault—Chocolates*. Archie would never run dry. The chocolates, for instance, were good for a dozen assignments.

Obie looked down at the field where the guys were skirmishing in the shadow of the goal posts. Sadness seized him. I should have gone out for football, he thought. He had wanted to—he'd been hot stuff with Pop Warner at St. Joe's. Instead, he had ended up as Secretary of The Vigils. Cool. But, hell, he couldn't even tell his parents about it.

"Know what, Archie?"

"What?"

"Life is sad, sometimes."

That was one of the great things about Archie, you could say things like that.

"Life is shit," Archie said.

The shadows of the goal posts definitely resembled a network of crosses, empty crucifixes. That's enough symbolism for one day, Obie told himself. If he hurried he could make the four o'clock bus to work.

Chapter 3

The girl was heart-wrenchingly, impossibly beautiful. Desire weakened his stomach. A waterfall of blond hair splashed on her bare shoulders. He studied the photograph surreptitiously and then closed the magazine and put it back where it belonged, on the top shelf. He glanced around to see if he'd been observed. The store owner positively prohibited the reading of magazines and a sign said No Buy No Read. But the owner was busy at the far end of the place.

Why did he always feel so guilty whenever he looked at *Playboy* and the other magazines? A lot of guys bought them, passed them around at school, hid them in the covers of notebooks, even resold them. He sometimes saw copies scattered casually on coffee tables in the homes of his friends. He had once bought a girlie magazine, paying for it with trembling fingers—a dollar and a quarter, his finances shot down in flames until his next allowance. And he didn't know what to do with the damn thing once it was in his possession. Sneaking it home on the bus, hiding it in the bottom drawer of his room, he was terrified of discovery. Finally, tired of smuggling it into the bathroom for swift perusals, and weary of his deceit, and haunted by the fear that his mother would find the magazine, Jerry had sneaked it out of the house and dropped it into a catchbasin. He listened to it splash dismally below, bidding a wistful farewell to the squandered buck and a quarter. A longing filled him. Would a girl ever love him? The one devastating sorrow he carried within him was the fear that he would die before holding a girl's breast in his hand.

Out at the bus stop, Jerry leaned against a telephone pole, body weary, echoing the assault of the football practices. For three days his body had absorbed punishment. But he was still on the roster, luckily. Idly, he watched the people on the Common across the street. He saw them every day. They were now part of the scenery like the Civil War Cannon and the World War Monuments, the flagpole. Hippies. Flower Children. Street People. Drifters. Drop-Outs. Everybody had a different name for them. They came out in the spring and stayed until October, hanging around, calling taunts to passersby occasionally but most of the time quiet, languid and peaceful. He was fascinated by them and sometimes envied their old clothes, their sloppiness, the way they didn't seem to give a damn about anything. Trinity was one of the last schools to retain a dress code— shirt and tie. He watched a cloud of smoke swirl around a girl in a floppy hat. Grass? He didn't know. A lot of things he didn't know.

Absorbed in his thoughts, he didn't notice that one of the street people had detached himself from the others and was crossing the street, dodging cars deftly.

"Hey, man."

Startled, Jerry realized the guy was addressing him. "Me?"

The fellow stood in the street, on the other side of a green Volkswagen, his chest resting on the car's roof. "Yes, you." He was about nineteen, long black hair brushing his shoulders, a curling mustache, like a limp black snake draped on his upper lip, the ends dangling near his chin. "You been staring at us, man, like every day. Standing here and staring."

They really say *man*, Jerry thought. He didn't think

anybody said *man* any more except as a joke. But this guy wasn't joking.

"Hey, man, you think we're in a zoo? That why you stare?"

"No. Look, I don't stare." But he did stare, every day.

"Yes, you do, man. You stand here and look at us. With your homework books and your nice shirt and your blue-and-white tie."

Jerry looked around uneasily. He confronted only strangers, nobody from school.

"We're not sub-humans, man."

"I didn't say you were."

"But you look it."

"Look," Jerry said, "I've got to get my bus." Which was ridiculous, of course, because the bus wasn't in sight.

"You know who's sub-human, man? You. You are. Going to school every day. And back home on the bus. And do your homework." The guy's voice was contemptuous. "Square boy. Middle-aged at fourteen, fifteen. Already caught in a routine. Wow."

A hiss and the stench of exhaust announced the arrival of the bus. Jerry swung away from the guy.

"Go get your bus, square boy," he called. "Don't miss the bus, boy. You're missing a lot of things in the world, better not miss that bus."

Jerry walked to the bus like a sleepwalker. He hated confrontations. His heart hammered. He climbed aboard, dropped his token in the coin box and lurched to his seat as the bus moved away from the curb.

He sat down, breathed deeply, closed his eyes.

Go get your bus, square boy.

He opened his eyes and slitted them against the invasion of the sun through the window.

You're missing a lot of things in the world, better not miss that bus.

A big put-on, of course. That was their specialty, people like that. Putting people on. Nothing else to do with their lives, piddling away their lives.

And yet . . .

Yet, what?

He didn't know. He thought of his life—going to school and coming home. Even though his tie was loose, dangling on his shirt, he yanked it off. He looked up at the advertising placards above the windows, wanting to turn his thoughts away from the confrontation.

Why? someone had scrawled in a blank space no advertiser had rented.

Why not? someone else had slashed in answer.

Jerry closed his eyes, exhausted suddenly, and it seemed like too much of an effort even to think.

Chapter 4

"How many boxes?"

"Twenty thousand."

Archie whistled in astonishment. He usually didn't blow his cool that easily, particularly with someone like Brother Leon. But the image of twenty thousand boxes of chocolates being delivered here to Trinity was ridiculous. Then he saw the mustache of moistness on Brother Leon's upper lip, the watery eyes and the dampness on his forehead. Something clicked. This wasn't the calm and deadly Leon who could hold a class in the palm of his hand. This was someone riddled with cracks and crevices. Archie became absolutely still, afraid that the rapid beating of his heart might betray his sudden knowledge, the proof of what he'd always suspected, not only of Brother Leon but most grownups, most adults: they were vulnerable, running scared, open to invasion.

"I know that's a lot of chocolates," Brother Leon admitted, managing to keep his voice casual, for which Archie admired him. A smart one, Leon, hard to pin down. Even though he was sweating like a madman, his voice remained calm, reasoned. "But we have tradition working in our favor. The chocolate sale is an annual event. The boys have come to expect it. If they can sell ten thousand boxes of chocolates in other years, why not twenty thousand this year? And these are special chocolates, Archie. High profit. A special deal."

"How is it special?" Archie asked, pressing his advantage, none of that student-talking-to-teacher crap in his voice. He was here in Leon's office by special invitation. Let Leon talk to the real Archie, not the kid who sat in his algebra class.

"Actually, these are Mother's Day chocolates. We were—that is, *I* was—able to pick them up at a bargain price. Beautiful boxes, gift boxes, and in perfect condition. They've been stored under the best of conditions since last spring. All we have to do is remove the purple ribbons that say *Mother* and we're in business. We can sell them for two dollars a box and make a profit of almost a dollar on each one."

"But twenty thousand boxes." Archie performed some quick calculations although he wasn't a whiz at math. "We're about four hundred guys in the school. That means everybody's got to sell fifty boxes. Usually, the guys have a quota of twenty-five boxes each to sell and the price is a dollar." He sighed. "Now, everything is doubled. That's a lot of selling for this school, Brother Leon. For any school."

"I know that, Archie. But Trinity is special, isn't it? If I didn't think the boys of Trinity could do it, do you think I would take a risk? Aren't we capable of what others aren't?"

Bullshit, was what Archie thought.

"I know what you're wondering, Archie—why am I burdening you with this problem?"

Archie, in fact, *was* wondering why Brother Leon had laid his plans before him. He had never been particularly friendly with Leon or any other Trinity teacher. And Leon was a special breed. On the surface, he was one of those pale, ingratiating kind of men who tiptoed through life on small, quick feet. He looked like a henpecked husband, a pushover, a sucker. He was the Assistant Headmaster of the school but actually served as a flunky for the Head. Like an errand boy. But all this was deceptive. In the classroom, Leon was another person altogether. Smirking, sarcastic. His thin, high voice venomous. He could hold your attention like a cobra. Instead of fangs, he used his teacher's pointer, flicking out here, there, everywhere. He watched the class like a hawk, suspicious, searching out cheaters or daydreamers, probing for weaknesses in the students and then exploiting those weaknesses. He had never taken on Archie. Not yet.

"Let me paint you the picture," Leon said, leaning forward in his chair. "All private schools, Catholic or otherwise, are struggling these days. Many are closing down. Prices are going up and we have only so many sources of income. As you know, Archie, we're not one of those exclusive boarding schools. And we don't have any wealthy alumni to draw on. We're a day school, dedicated to preparing young men from middle class homes for college. There are no rich men's sons here. Take yourself, for instance. Your father operates an insurance agency. He makes a good salary but he's hardly wealthy, is he? Take Tommy Desjardins. His father's a dentist—very well off, they have two cars, a summer home—and that's about tops for the parents of Trinity boys." He held up his hand. "I'm not trying to put down the parents." Archie winced. It irritated him when grownups resorted to student language like *put down*. "What I'm saying, Archie, is that the parents are mostly in modest circumstances and can't absorb any more tuition increases. We have to find revenue wherever possible. Football barely pays for itself—we haven't had a winning season for three years. The interest in boxing has fallen off now that television doesn't feature boxing anymore . . ."

Archie stifled a yawn—so what else was new?

"I'm putting my cards on the table, Archie, to show

you, to impress upon you, how we have to tap every source of income, how even a chocolate sale can be vital and important to us . . ."

Silence fell. The school was hushed around them, so hushed that Archie wondered whether the office was soundproof. Classes were over for the day, of course, but that was the time when a lot of other action got started. Particularly Vigil action.

"Another thing," Leon went on. "We've kept this quiet but the Head is ill, perhaps seriously so. He's scheduled to enter the hospital tomorrow. Tests and things. The outlook isn't good . . ."

Archie waited for Leon to get to the point. Was he going to make a ridiculous pitch for the chocolate sale to be a success in honor of the sick Headmaster? "Win one for The Gipper" like some pukey late-night movie?

"He may be incapacitated for weeks."

"That's rough." So what?

"Which means—the school will be in my charge. The school will be my responsibility."

The silence again. But this time Archie felt a waiting in the silence. He had a feeling that Leon was about to make his point.

"I need your help, Archie."

"My help?" Archie asked, feigning surprise, trying to keep any trace of mockery out of his voice. He knew now why he was here. Leon didn't mean Archie's help—he meant the help of The Vigils. And didn't dare put it into words. No one was allowed to breathe a word about The Vigils. Officially, The Vigils did not exist. How could a school condone an organization like The Vigils? The school allowed it to function by ignoring it completely, pretending it wasn't there. But it was there, all right, Archie thought bitterly. It was there because it served a purpose. The Vigils kept things under control. Without The Vigils, Trinity might have been torn apart like other schools had been, by demonstrations, protests, all that crap. Archie was surprised by Leon's audacity, knowing his connection with The Vigils and bringing him in here this way.

"But how can *I* help?" Archie asked, turning the screw, emphasizing the singular of himself and not the plural of The Vigils.

"By getting behind the sale. As you said, Archie— twenty thousand boxes, that's a lot of chocolates."

"The price is doubled, too," Archie reminded him, enjoying himself now. "Two dollars a box, instead of one."

"But we need that money desperately."

"How about the bonus? The school always gives the boys a bonus."

"As usual, Archie. A day off from school when every chocolate has been sold."

"No free trip this year? Last year we were taken to Boston to a stage show." Archie didn't care about the trip but he enjoyed this reverse position—himself asking the questions and Leon squirming, so different from the classroom.

"I'll think of something as a substitute," Leon said.

Archie let the silence stretch.

"Can I count on you, Archie?" Leon's forehead was damp again.

Archie decided to plunge. To see how far he could go. "But what can I do? I'm just one guy."

"You have influence, Archie."

"Influence?" Archie's voice was coming out loud and clear. He was cool. In command. Let Leon sweat. Archie was sweet and cool. "I'm not a class officer.

I'm not a member of the Student Council." Christ, if only the guys were here to see him. "I don't even make the Honor Roll . . ."

Suddenly, Leon wasn't sweating anymore. The beads of perspiration still danced on his forehead but he had become stiff and cold. Archie could feel the coldness—more than cold, an icy hate coming across the desk like a deadly ray from some bleak and lethal planet. Have I gone too far, he wondered. I've got this guy for algebra, my weakest subject.

"You know what I mean," Leon said, his voice like a door slamming.

Their eyes met, held. A showdown now? At this moment? Would that be the smart thing to do? Archie believed in always doing the smart thing. Not the thing you ached to do, not the impulsive act, but the thing that would pay off later. That's why he was The Assigner. That's why The Vigils depended on him. Hell, The Vigils *were* the school. And he, Archie Costello, was The Vigils. That's why Leon had called him here, that's why Leon was practically begging for his help. Archie suddenly had a terrific craving for a Hershey.

"I know what you mean," Archie said, postponing the showdown. Leon could be like money in the bank, for future use.

"You'll help, then?"

"I'll check with them," Archie said, letting *them* hang in the air.

And it hung.

Leon didn't pick it up.

Neither did Archie.

They looked at each other for a long moment.

"The Vigils will help," Archie said, unable to contain himself any longer. He had never been able to use those words—The Vigils—aloud to a teacher, had

had to deny the existence of the organization for so long that it was beautiful to use them, to see the surprise on Leon's pale perspiring face.

Then he pushed back his chair and left the office without waiting for the teacher's dismissal.

Chapter 5

"Your name is Goubert?"

"Yes."

"They call you The Goober?"

"Yes."

"Yes, what?"

Archie was disgusted with himself even as he said it. *Yes, what?* like a scene from out of an old World War Two movie. But the kid Goubert stammered and then said, "Yes, *sir.*" Like a raw recruit.

"Know why you're here, Goober?"

The Goober hesitated. Despite his height, he was easily six-one, he reminded Archie of a child, someone who didn't belong here, as if he'd been caught sneaking into an Adults Only movie. He was too skinny, of course. And he had the look of a loser. Vigil bait.

"Yes, sir," The Goober finally said.

Archie was always puzzled about whatever there was inside of him that enjoyed these performances— toying with kids, leading them on, humiliating them, finally. He'd earned the job of Assigner because of his quick mind, his swift intelligence, his fertile imagination, his ability to see two moves ahead as if life were a giant checker or chess game. But something more than that, something nobody could find words to describe. Archie knew what it was and recognized it, although it eluded a definition. One night while watching an old Marx Brothers movie on the Late Show, he was held entranced by a scene where the brothers were searching for a missing painting. Groucho said, "We'll search every room in the house." Chico asked, "But what if it ain't in the house?" Groucho replied, "Then we'll search the house next door." "What if there ain't no house next door?" And Groucho, "Then we'll build one." And they immediately started to draw up plans for building the house. That's what Archie did—built the house nobody could anticipate a need for, except himself, a house that was invisible to everyone else.

"If you know, then tell me why you're here, Goober," Archie said now, his voice gentle. He always treated them with tenderness, as if a bond existed between them.

Someone snickered. Archie stiffened, shot a look at Carter, a withering look that said, tell them to cut the crap. Carter snapped his fingers, which sounded in the quiet storage room like the banging of a gavel. The Vigils were grouped as usual in a circle around Archie and the kid receiving the assignment. The small room behind the gym was windowless with only one door leading to the gymnasium itself: a perfect spot for Vigil meetings—private, the solitary entrance easily guarded, and dim, lit by a single bulb dangling from the ceiling, a 40-watt bulb that bestowed only a feeble light on the proceedings. The silence was deafening after the snap of Carter's fingers. Nobody fooled around with Carter. Carter was the president of The Vigils because the president was always a football player—the muscle someone like Archie needed. But everyone knew that the head of The Vigils was The Assigner, Archie Costello, who was always one step ahead of them all.

The Goober looked frightened. He was one of those kids who always wanted to please everybody.

The guy who never got the girl but worshipped her in secret while the big shot hero rode off in the sunset with her in the end.

"Tell me," Archie said, "why you're here." He allowed a bit of impatience to appear in his voice.

"For . . . an assignment."

"Do you realize that there's nothing personal in the assignment?"

The Goober nodded.

"That this is tradition here at Trinity?"

"Yes."

"And that you must pledge silence?"

"Yes," The Goober said, swallowing, his Adam's apple doing a dance in that long thin neck.

Silence.

Archie let it gather. He could feel a heightening of interest in the room. It always happened this way when an assignment was about to be given. He knew what they were thinking—what's Archie come up with this time? Sometimes Archie resented them. The members of The Vigils did nothing but enforce the rules. Carter was muscle and Obie an errand boy. Archie alone was always under pressure, devising the assignments, working them out. As if he was some kind of machine. Press a button: out comes an assignment. What did they know about the agonies of it all? The nights he tossed and turned? The times he felt used up, empty? And yet he couldn't deny that he exulted in moments like this, the guys leaning forward in anticipation, the mystery that surrounded them all, the kid Goober white-faced and frightened, the place so quiet you could almost hear your own heartbeat. And all eyes on him: Archie.

"Goober."

"Yes, yes sir." Swallow.

"Know what a screwdriver is?"

"Yes."

"Can you put your hands on one?"

"Yes, yes sir. My father. He has a tool chest."

"Fine. Know what they use screwdrivers for, Goober?"

"Yes."

"What for?"

"To screw things . . . I mean, to put screws into things."

Someone laughed. And Archie let it pass. A relief to the tension.

"And also, Goober," Archie said, "a screwdriver takes screws out of things. Right?"

"Yes, sir."

"A screwdriver, then, can loosen as well as tighten, right?"

"Right," The Goober said, nodding his head, eager, his attention fastened on the thought of the screwdriver, almost as if he were hypnotized, and Archie was carried on marvelous waves of power and glory, leading The Goober toward the ultimate destination, feeding him the information little by little, the best part of the lousy job. Not really lousy, though. Great, in fact. Beautiful, in fact. Worth all the sweat.

"Now, do you know where Brother Eugene's homeroom is located?"

The anticipation in the air was almost visible at this moment, blazing, electric.

"Yes. Room nineteen. Second floor."

"Right!" Archie said, as if giving The Goober an *A* for recitation. "Next Thursday afternoon, you'll make arrangements to be free. Afternoon, evening, all night, if necessary."

The Goober stood there, spellbound.

"The school will be deserted. The brothers, most of

them, the ones who count, will be off to a conference at Provincial headquarters in Maine. The janitor is taking a day off. There'll be no one in the building after three in the afternoon. No one but you, Goober. You and your screwdriver."

Now, the final moment, the climax, almost like coming—

"And here's what you do, Goober." Pause. "You loosen."

"Loosen?" The Adam's apple dancing.

"Loosen."

Archie waited a beat—in strict command of the room, the silence almost unbearable—and said, "Everything in Brother Eugene's room is held together by screws. The chairs, the desks, the blackboards. Now, with your little screwdriver—maybe you'd better bring along various and assorted sizes, just in case—you start to loosen. Don't take out the screws. Just loosen them until they reach that point where they're almost ready to fall out, everything hanging there by a thread . . ."

A howl of delight came from the guys—probably Obie, who had gotten the picture, who could see the house that Archie was building, the house that didn't exist until he built it in their minds. Then, others joined in the laughter as they envisioned the result of the assignment. Archie let himself be caressed by the laughter of admiration, knowing that he'd scored again. They were always waiting for him to fail, to fall flat on his face, but he'd scored once more.

"Jeez," The Goober said. "That's going to take a lot of work. There's a lot of desks and chairs in there."

"You'll have all night. We guarantee you won't be disturbed."

"Jeez." The Adam's apple was positively convulsive now.

"Thursday," Archie said, a command in his voice, no nonsense, final, irrevocable.

The Goober nodded, accepting the assignment like a sentence of doom, the way all the others did, knowing there was no way out, no reprieve, no appeal. The law of The Vigils was final, everyone at Trinity knew that.

Somebody whispered, "Wow."

Carter snapped his fingers again and tension quickly built up in the room once more. But a different kind of tension. Tension with teeth in it. For Archie. He braced himself.

Reaching under the abandoned teacher's desk he sat behind as presiding officer, Carter pulled out a small black box. He shook it and the sound of marbles could be heard clicking together inside. Obie came forward, holding a key in his hand. Was that a smile on Obie's face? Archie couldn't be sure. He wondered, does Obie really hate me? Do they all hate me? Not that it mattered. Not while Archie held the power. He would conquer all, even the black box.

Carter took the key from Obie and held it up.

"Ready?" he asked Archie.

"Ready," Archie said, keeping his face expressionless, inscrutable as usual, even though he felt a bead of perspiration trace a cold path from his armpit to his rib. The black box was his nemesis. It contained six marbles: five of them white and one of them black. It was an ingenious idea thought up by someone long before Archie's time, someone who was wise enough—or a bastard enough—to realize that an assigner could go off the deep end if there wasn't some kind of control. The box provided the control. After every assignment, it was presented to Archie. If Archie drew a white marble, the assignment stood as ordered. If Archie drew the black marble, it would be necessary for Archie himself to carry out the assignment, to perform the duty he had assigned for others.

He had beaten the black box for three years—could he do it again? Or was his luck running out? Would the law of averages catch up to him? A tremor ran along his arm as he extended his hand toward the box. He hoped no one had noticed. Reaching inside, he grabbed a marble, concealed it in the palm of his hand. He withdrew his hand, held the arm straight out, calmly now, without shiver or tremor. He opened his hand. The marble was white.

The corner of Archie's mouth twitched as the tension of his body relaxed. He had beaten them again. He had won again. I am Archie. I cannot lose.

Carter snapped his fingers and the meeting began to break up. Suddenly, Archie felt empty, used up, discarded. He looked at the kid Goober who stood there in bewilderment, looking as if he were going to cry. Archie almost felt sorry for the kid. Almost. But not quite.

Chapter 6

Brother Leon was getting ready to put on his show. Jerry knew the symptoms—all the guys knew them. Most of them were freshmen and had been in Leon's class only a month or so but the teacher's pattern had already emerged. First, Leon gave them a reading assignment. Then he'd pace up and down, up and down, restless, sighing, wandering through the aisles, the blackboard pointer poised in his hand, the pointer he used either like a conductor's baton or a musketeer's sword. He'd use the tip to push around a book on a desk or to flick a kid's necktie, scratching gently down some guy's back, poking the pointer as if he were a rubbish collector picking his way through the debris of the classroom. One day, the pointer had rested on Jerry's head for a moment, and then passed on. Unaccountably, Jerry had shivered, as if he had just escaped some terrible fate.

Now, aware of Leon prowling ceaselessly around the classroom, Jerry kept his eyes on paper although he didn't feel like reading. Two more periods. He looked forward to football practice. After days of calisthenics, the coach had said that probably he'd let them use the ball this afternoon.

"Enough of this crap."

That was Brother Leon—always trying to shock. Using words like crap and bull and slipping in a few damns and hells once in a while. Actually, he did shock. Maybe because the words were so startling as they issued from this pale and inoffensive looking little man. Later on, you found out that he wasn't inoffensive, of course. Now, everyone looked up at Leon as that word crap echoed in the room. Ten minutes left—time enough for Leon to perform, to play one of his games. The class looked at him in a kind of horrible fascination.

The brother's glance went slowly around the room, like the ray of a lighthouse sweeping a familiar coast, searching for hidden defects. Jerry felt a sense of dread and anticipation, both at the same time.

"Bailey," Leon said.

"Yes, Brother Leon." Leon *would* pick Bailey: one of the weak kids, high honor student, but shy, introverted, always reading, his eyes red-rimmed behind the glasses.

"Up here," Leon said, finger beckoning.

Bailey went quietly to the front of the room. Jerry could see a vein throbbing in the boy's temple.

"As you know, gentlemen," Brother Leon began, addressing the class directly and ignoring Bailey completely although the boy was standing beside him, "as you know, a certain discipline must be maintained in a school. A line must be drawn between teachers and students. We teachers would love to be one of the boys, of course. But that line of separation must remain. An invisible line, perhaps, but still there." His moist eyes gleamed. "After all, you can't see the wind but it's there. You see its handiwork, bending the trees, stirring the leaves . . ."

As he spoke he gestured, his arm becoming the wind, the pointer in his hand following the direction of the wind and suddenly, without warning, striking Bailey on the cheek. The boy leaped backward in pain and surprise.

"Bailey, I'm sorry," Leon said, but his voice lacked apology. Had it been an accident? Or another of Leon's little cruelties?

Now all eyes were on the stricken Bailey. Brother Leon studied him, looking at him as if he were a specimen under a microscope, as if the specimen contained the germ of some deadly disease. You had to hand it to Leon—he was a superb actor. He loved to read short stories aloud, taking all the parts, providing all the sound effects. Nobody yawned or fell asleep in Leon's class. You had to be alert every minute, just as everyone was alert now, looking at Bailey, wondering what Leon's next move would be. Under Leon's steady gaze, Bailey had stopped stroking his cheek, even though a pink welt had appeared, like an evil stain spreading on his flesh. Somehow, the tables were turned. Now it seemed as if Bailey had been at fault all along, that Bailey had committed an error, had stood in the wrong place at the wrong time and had caused his own misfortune. Jerry squirmed in his chair. Leon gave him the creeps, the way he could change the atmosphere in a room without even speaking a word.

"Bailey," Leon said. But not looking at Bailey, looking at the class as if they were all in on a joke that Bailey knew nothing about. As if the class and Leon were banded together in a secret conspiracy.

"Yes, Brother Leon?" Bailey asked, his eyes magnified behind the glasses.

A pause.

"Bailey," Brother Leon said. "Why do you find it necessary to cheat?"

They say the hydrogen bomb makes no noise: there's only a blinding white flash that strikes cities dead. The noise comes after the flash, after the silence. That's the kind of silence that blazed in the classroom now.

Bailey stood speechless, his mouth an open wound.

"Is silence an admission of guilt, Bailey?" Brother

Leon asked, turning to the boy at last.

Bailey shook his head frantically. Jerry felt his own head shaking, joining Bailey in silent denial.

"Ah, Bailey," Leon sighed, his voice fluttering with sadness. "What are we going to do about you?" Turning toward the class again, buddies with them— him and the class against the cheat.

"I don't cheat, Brother Leon," Bailey said, his voice a kind of squeak.

"But look at the evidence, Bailey. Your marks—all A's, no less. Every test, every paper, every homework assignment. Only a genius is capable of that sort of performance. Do you claim to be a genius, Bailey?" Toying with him. "I'll admit you look like one—those glasses, that pointed chin, that wild hair . . ."

Leon leaned toward the class, tossing his own chin, awaiting the approval of laughter, everything in his manner suggesting the response of laughter from the class. And it came. They laughed. Hey, what's going on here, Jerry wondered even as he laughed with them. Because Bailey did somehow look like a genius or at least a caricature of the mad scientists in old movies.

"Bailey," Brother Leon said, turning his full attention to the boy again as the laughter subsided.

"Yes," Bailey replied miserably.

"You haven't answered my question." He walked deliberately to the window and was suddenly absorbed in the street outside, the September leaves turning brown and crisp.

Bailey stood alone at the front of the class, as if he was facing a firing squad. Jerry felt his cheeks getting warm, throbbing with the warmth.

"Well, Bailey?" From Leon at the window, still intent on the world outside.

"I don't cheat, Brother Leon," Bailey said, a surge

of strength in his voice, like he was taking a last stand.

"Then how do you account for all those A's?"

"I don't know."

Brother Leon whirled around. "Are you perfect, Bailey? All those A's—that implies perfection. Is that the answer, Bailey?"

For the first time, Bailey looked at the class itself, in mute appeal, like something wounded, lost, abandoned.

"Only God is perfect, Bailey."

Jerry's neck began to hurt. And his lungs burned. He realized he'd been holding his breath. He gulped air, carefully, not wanting to move a muscle. He wished he was invisible. He wished he wasn't here in the classroom. He wanted to be out on the football field, fading back, looking for a receiver.

"Do you compare yourself with God, Bailey?"

Cut it out, Brother, cut it out, Jerry cried silently.

"If God is perfect and you are perfect, Bailey, does that suggest something to you?"

Bailey didn't answer, eyes wide in disbelief. The class was utterly silent. Jerry could hear the hum of the electric clock—he'd never realized before that electric clocks hummed.

"The other alternative, Bailey, is that you are not perfect. And, of course, you're not." Leon's voice softened. "I know you wouldn't consider anything so sacrilegious."

"That's right, Brother Leon," Bailey said, relieved.

"Which leaves us with only one conclusion," Leon said, his voice bright and triumphant, as if he had made an important discovery. "You cheat!"

In that moment, Jerry hated Brother Leon. He could taste the hate in his stomach—it was acid, foul, burning.

"You're a cheat, Bailey. And a liar." The words like whips.

You rat, Jerry thought. You bastard.

A voice boomed from the rear of the classroom. "Aw, let the kid alone."

Leon whipped around. "Who said that?" His moist eyes glistened.

The bell rang, ending the period. Feet scuffled as the boys pushed back their chairs, preparing to leave, to get out of that terrible place.

"Wait a minute," Brother Leon said. Softly—but heard by everyone. "Nobody moves."

The students settled in their chairs again.

Brother Leon regarded them pityingly, shaking his head, a sad and dismal smile on his lips. "You poor fools," he said. "You idiots. Do you know who's the best one here? The bravest of all?" He placed his hand on Bailey's shoulder. "Gregory Bailey, that's who. He denied cheating. He stood up to my accusations. He stood his ground! But you, gentlemen, you sat there and enjoyed yourselves. And those of you who didn't enjoy yourselves allowed it to happen, allowed me to proceed. You turned this classroom into Nazi Germany for a few moments. Yes, yes, someone finally protested. *Aw, let the kid alone.*" Mimicking the deep voice perfectly. "A feeble protest, too little and too late." There was scuffling in the corridors, students waiting to enter. Leon ignored the noise. He turned to Bailey, touched the top of his head with the pointer as if he were bestowing knighthood. "You did well, Bailey. I'm proud of you. You passed the biggest test of all—you were true to yourself." Bailey's chin was wobbling all over the place. "Of course you don't cheat, Bailey," his voice tender and paternal. He gestured toward the class—he was a great one for gestures. "Your classmates out there. They're the cheaters. They cheated you today. They're the ones who doubted you—I never did."

Leon went to his desk. "Dismissed," he said, his voice filled with contempt for all of them.

Chapter 7

"What're you doing, Emile?" Archie asked, amusement in his voice. The amusement was there because it was obvious what Emile Janza was doing—he was siphoning gas from a car, watching it flow into a glass jug.

Emile giggled. He, too, was amused that Archie should have discovered him performing such an act.

"I'm getting my gas for the week," Emile said.

The car, parked at the far end of the school's parking lot, belonged to a senior by the name of Carlson.

"What would you do, Emile, if Carlson came along and saw you stealing his gas?" Archie asked, although he knew the answer.

Emile didn't bother to reply. He grinned knowingly at Archie. Carlson wouldn't do anything about it at all. He was a thin, mild kid who hated getting involved in messes. Not too many people defied Emile Janza, anyway, whether they were fat or skinny, mild or not. Emile was a brute which was kind of funny because he didn't look like a brute. He wasn't big or overly strong. In fact, he was small for a tackle on the football team. But he was an animal and he didn't play by the rules. Not if he could help it. His small eyes were imbedded in pale flesh, eyes that seldom smiled despite the giggle and the grin that sometimes flashed across his face, especially when he knew he was reaching people. That's what Emile Janza called it—reaching people. Like whistling softly in class so that it got on the teacher's nerves, a barely perceptible whistle that could drive a teacher up the wall. That's why Emile Janza reversed the usual process. Wise guys usually sat in back. Emile didn't. He chose seats near the front where he'd be in better position to harass the teacher. Whistling, grunting, belching, tapping his foot, stirring restlessly, sniffling. Hell, if you did that kind of stuff from the back of the room the teacher wouldn't notice.

But Emile didn't harass only teachers. He found that the world was full of willing victims, especially kids his own age. He had discovered a truth early in life—in the fourth grade, in fact. Nobody wanted trouble, nobody wanted to make trouble, nobody wanted a showdown. The knowledge was a revelation. It opened doors. You could take a kid's lunch or even his lunch money and nothing usually happened because most kids wanted peace at any price. Of course, you have to choose your victims carefully because there were exceptions. Those who protested found that it was easier to let Emile have his way. Who wanted to get hurt? Later, Emile stumbled upon another truth, although it was hard to put into words. He found that people had a fear of being embarrassed or humiliated, of being singled out for special attention. Like in a bus. You could call out to a kid, especially one who blushes easily, and say, "Jeez, you got bad breath, know that? Don't you ever brush your teeth?" Even if the kid had the sweetest breath in the world. Or, "Did you lay a fart, kid? What a dirty thing to do." Softly, but loud enough for everybody to hear. Stuff like that—in the cafeteria, during lunch, in study class. But it was better in public places, with strangers nearby, especially girls. That's when the kids squirmed. As a result, people went around being extra nice to Emile Janza. And Emile basked in that treatment. Emile was not stupid but he was not exactly bright in class. However, he managed to squeak by—no *F*'s, only a couple of *D*'s, all of which satisfied his father whom Emile regarded as stupid and whose major dream was to have his son graduate from a fancy private school like Trinity. His father didn't know how cruddy the place was.

"Emile, you're a beautiful person," Archie said as Emile, satisfied with the overflowing glass jug, carefully screwed the cap of the gas tank on.

Emile looked up suspiciously, on guard. He was never sure whether Archie Costello was serious or not. Emile never fooled around with Archie. In fact, Archie was one of the few people in the world Emile respected. Maybe even feared. Archie and The Vigils.

"Did you say beautiful?"

Archie laughed. "I mean, Emile, you're something special. Who else would siphon gas in the middle of the day? Out in the open like this? Beautiful."

Emile smiled at Archie, suddenly wistful. He wished he could share with Archie some of the other stuff. But he couldn't. Somehow, it was too private but often he wanted to tell people about it. How he got a kick out of things. For instance, when he went to the john at school, he seldom flushed the toilet—and got a kick out of picturing the next kid who'd go in and find the mess in the bowl. Crazy. And if you told anybody, it would be hard to explain. Like how he sometimes felt actually horny when he roughhoused a kid or tackled a guy viciously in football and gave him an extra jab when he had him on the ground. How could you tell anybody about that? And yet he felt that Archie would understand. Birds of a feather, that was it. Despite that picture. The picture that haunted his life.

Archie began to walk away.

"Hey, Archie, where're you going?"

"I don't want to be an accessory, Emile."

Emile laughed. "Carlson's not gonna press charges."

Archie shook his head in admiration. "Beautiful," he said.

"Hey, Archie. How about the picture?"

"Yes, Emile. How *about* the picture?"

"You know what I mean."

"Beautiful," Archie said, walking away quickly now, wanting to keep Emile Janza sweating about the picture. Actually, Archie hated people like Janza even though he could admire their handiwork. People like Janza were animals. But they came in handy. Janza and the picture—like money in the bank.

Emile Janza watched the departing figure of Archie Costello. Someday, he'd be like Archie—cool, a member of The Vigils. Emile kicked at the rear tire of Carlson's car. Somehow he was disappointed that Carlson hadn't caught him siphoning the gas.

Chapter 8

The Goober was beautiful when he ran. His long arms and legs moved flowingly and flawlessly, his body floating as if his feet weren't touching the ground. When he ran, he forgot about his acne and his awkwardness and the shyness that paralyzed him when a girl looked his way. Even his thoughts became sharper, and things were simple and uncomplicated—he could solve math problems when he ran or memorize football play patterns. Often he rose early in the morning, before anyone else, and poured himself liquid through the sunrise streets, and everything seemed beautiful, everything in its proper orbit, nothing impossible, the entire world attainable.

When he ran, he even loved the pain, the hurt of the running, the burning in his lungs and the spasms that sometimes gripped his calves. He loved it because he knew he could endure the pain, and even go beyond it. He had never pushed himself to the limit but he felt all this reserve strength inside of him: more than strength actually—determination. And it sang in him as he ran, his heart pumping blood joyfully through his body. He'd gone out for football and there was a good feeling when he caught one of Jerry Renault's passes and outran everybody for a score. But it was the running he loved. The neighbors would see him waterfalling down High Street, carried by the momentum of his speed, and they'd cry out, "Going for the Olympics, Goob?" Or, "Got your eye on the world record, Goob?" And on he'd run, floating, flowing.

But he wasn't running now. He was in Brother Eugene's homeroom and he was terrified. He was fifteen years old and six-one-and-a-half and too old to cry but tears blurred his vision, as if the room was under water. He was ashamed and disgusted with himself but he couldn't help it. The tears were from frustration as well as terror. And the terror was different from any other kind he'd ever known: the terror of a walking nightmare. Like waking up from a bad dream in which a monster was gaining on you and breathing a sigh of relief as you realized you were safe in your bed and then looking toward the moonlit doorway and seeing the monster stalking toward your bed. And knowing you'd stumbled from one nightmare into another—and how do you find your way back to the real world?

He knew that he was in the real world at this moment, of course. Everything was real enough. The screwdrivers and the pliers were real. So were the desks and chairs and the blackboards. So was the world outside, a world he had been shut away from since three o'clock this afternoon when he had sneaked into the school. Now the world had changed, had grown blurred with day's leaving and then purple at dusk and then dark. It was now nine o'clock and The Goober sat on the floor, his head against a desk, angry at his damp cheeks. His eyes stung from strain. The Vigils said he was allowed to put on the small emergency night light each classroom was furnished. A flashlight was forbidden because it might look suspicious to outsiders. The Goober had found the job almost impossible. He had been in the classroom six hours and had only finished two rows of desks and chairs. The screws were stubborn, most of them factory-tight, resisting the twists of the screwdriver.

I'll never get done, he thought. I'll be here all night

and my folks will go crazy and it still won't be done. He envisioned himself being discovered here tomorrow morning, collapsed in exhaustion, a disgrace to himself and The Vigils and the school. He was hungry and had a headache and felt that everything would be all right if he could only get out of here and run, hurtle himself through the streets, free from the terrible assignment.

A noise from the corridor. That was another thing—it was spooky. All kinds of noises. The walls spoke their own creaky language, the floors crackled, motors hummed somewhere, the humming almost human. Enough to scare a guy to death. He hadn't been this scared since he was just a kid and woke up in the middle of the night calling for his mother.

Thump. There—another noise. He looked with dread toward the doorway, not wanting to look but unable to resist the temptation, remembering his old nightmare.

"Hey, Goober," the whisper came.

"Who's there?" he whispered back. Relief swept him. He wasn't alone anymore, someone else was here.

"How're you doing?"

A figure was advancing toward him on all fours, like an animal. The aspect of the beast—nightmare, after all. He shrank back, his skin hot and prickly, like the onset of hives. He was aware of other figures crawling into the room, knees scraping across the floor. The first figure was now in front of him.

"Need some help?"

The Goober squinted. The kid was masked.

"It's going slow," Goober said.

The masked figure grabbed the front of Goober's shirt and twisted hard, pulling him forward. He could smell pizza on the kid's breath. The mask was black, the kind Zorro wore in the movies.

"Listen, Goubert. The assignment is more important than anything else, understand? More important than you, me or the school. That's why we're going to give you some help. To get the thing done right." The kid's knuckles dug hard into Goober's chest. "You tell anybody about this and you're through at Trinity. Got that?"

Goober gulped and nodded. His throat was dry. He was happy beyond belief. Help had arrived. The impossible had become possible.

The masked figure raised his head. "Okay, fellows, let's get going."

One of the other fellows raised his face, also masked, and said, "This is a gas."

"Shut up and get to work," the guy who was obviously the leader said.

He also let go of Goober's shirt and pulled out his own screwdriver.

It took them three hours.

Chapter 9

Jerry's mother had died in the spring. They had been staying up with her nights—his father and some of his uncles and aunts and Jerry himself—since her return from the hospital. They came and went in shifts that final week, everyone exhausted and mute with sadness. Nothing more could be done for her at the hospital and she was taken home to die. She'd loved her home so much, always had some project underway—wallpapering, painting, refinishing furniture. "Give me twenty workers like her and I'd open a small factory and make a million," his father used to joke. And then she got sick. And died. Watching her ebb away, seeing her beauty diminish, witnessing the awful alteration of her face and body was too much for Jerry to bear and he sometimes fled her bedroom, ashamed of his weakness, avoiding his father. Jerry wished he could be as strong as his father, always in control, masking his sorrow and grief. When his mother finally died, suddenly, at three-thirty in the afternoon, slipping off quietly without a murmur, Jerry was overcome with rage, a fiery anger that found him standing at her coffin in silent fury. He was angry at the way the disease had ravaged her. He was angry at his inability to do anything about saving her. His anger was so deep and sharp in him that it drove out sorrow. He wanted to bellow at the world, cry out against her death, topple buildings, split the earth open, tear down trees. And he did nothing except lie awake in the dark, thinking of her body there in the funeral home, not her anymore, but a *thing* suddenly, cold and pale. His father was a stranger during those terrible days, like a sleepwalker going through the motions, like a puppet being maneuvered by invisible strings. Jerry felt hopeless and abandoned, all tight inside. Even at the cemetery, they stood apart from each other, a huge distance between them even though they were side by side. But not touching. And then, at the end of the service, as they turned to leave, Jerry found himself in his father's arms, his face pressed close to his father's body, smelling the cigarette tobacco, the faint odor of peppermint mouthwash, that familiar smell that was his father. There in the cemetery, clinging to each other in mutual sorrow and loss, the tears came for both of them. Jerry didn't know where his own tears began and his father's left off. They wept without shame, out of a nameless need, and walked together afterward, arm in arm, toward the waiting car. The fiery knot of anger had come undone, unraveled, and Jerry realized as they drove back from the cemetery that something worse had taken its place—emptiness, a yawning cavity like a hole in his chest.

That was the last moment of intimacy he and his father had shared. The routine of school for himself, and work for his father, had been taken up and they both threw themselves into it. His father sold the house and they moved to a garden apartment where no memories lurked around corners. Jerry spent most of the summer in Canada, on the farm of a distant cousin. He had fallen into the routine of the farm willingly, hoping to build up his body for Trinity and football in the fall. His mother had been born in that small Canadian town. There was a kind of comfort walking the narrow streets where she herself had walked as a girl. When he returned to New England in late August, he and his father fell into a simple routine. Work and school. And football. On the field, bruised and battered or grimy and dirty, Jerry felt as if he was part of something. And he sometimes wondered, what was his father part of?

He thought of that now as he looked at his father. He'd come from school to find his father napping on a sofa in the den, arms folded across his chest. Jerry moved soundlessly through the apartment, not wanting to awaken the sleeping figure. His father was a pharmacist and worked all kinds of staggered hours for a chain of drugstores in the area. His work often included night shifts which meant broken sleep. As a result, he'd developed the habit of falling off into naps whenever he found a moment to relax. Jerry's stomach was weak from hunger but he sat quietly down across from his father now, waiting for him to waken. He was weary from practice, the constant punishment his body took, the frustration of never getting a play off, never completing a pass, the coach's sarcasm, the lingering September heat.

Watching his father sleep, the face relaxed in slumber, all the harsh lines of age less defined, he remembered hearing that people who had been married a long time began to resemble each other. He squinted his eyes, the way one inspects a fine painting, searching for his mother there in the face of his father. And, without warning, the anguish of her loss returned, like a blow to his stomach, and he was afraid that he would faint. Through some nightmarish miracle, he was able to superimpose the image of his mother's face on his father's—and for a moment the echo of all her sweetness was there and he had to go through all the horror of visualizing her in the coffin again.

His father awakened, as if slapped from sleep by an

invisible hand. The vision vanished and Jerry leaped to his feet.

"Hi, Jerry," his father said, rubbing his eyes, sitting up. His hair wasn't even mussed. But then how could a stiff crew cut get mussed up? "Have a good day, Jerry?"

His father's voice restored normalcy. "Okay, I guess. Another practice. One of these days, I'll get a pass off."

"Fine."

"How was your day, Dad?"

"Fine."

"That's good."

"Mrs. Hunter left us a casserole. Tuna fish. She said you liked it fine last time."

Mrs. Hunter was the housekeeper. She spent every afternoon cleaning up the place and preparing some kind of evening meal for them. She was a gray-haired woman who constantly embarrassed Jerry because she insisted on tousling his hair and murmuring, "Child, child . . ." like he was a third grader or something.

"Hungry, Jerry? I can get it ready in five or ten minutes. Heat the oven and there it is . . ."

"Fine."

He was throwing one of his father's *fines* back at him although his father didn't notice. That was his father's favorite word—fine.

"Hey, Dad."

"Yes, Jerry?"

"Were things really fine at the store today?"

His father paused near the kitchen doorway, puzzled. "What do you mean, Jerry?"

"I mean, every day I ask you how things are going and every day you say fine. Don't you have some *great* days? Or *rotten* days?"

"A drugstore's pretty much the same all the time, Jerry. The prescriptions come in and we fill them—and that's about it. You fill them carefully, taking all precautions, double-checking. It's true what they say about doctors' handwriting, but I've told you that before." He was frowning now, as if searching his memory, trying to find something that would please the boy. "There was that attempted holdup three years ago—the time that drug addict came in like a wild man."

Jerry made an effort to hide his shock and disappointment. Was that the most exciting thing that had ever happened to his father? That pathetic holdup try by a scared young kid brandishing a toy pistol? Was life that dull, that boring and humdrum for people? He hated to think of his own life stretching ahead of him that way, a long succession of days and nights that were fine, *fine*—not good, not bad, not great, not lousy, not exciting, not anything.

He followed his father into the kitchen. The casserole slid into the oven like a letter into a mailbox. Jerry wasn't hungry suddenly, all appetite gone. "How about a salad?" his father asked. "I think there's lettuce and stuff around."

Jerry nodded automatically. Was this all there was to life, after all? You finished school, found an occupation, got married, became a father, watched your wife die, and then lived through days and nights that seemed to have no sunrises, no dawns and no dusks, nothing but a gray drabness. Or was he being fair to his father? To himself? Wasn't each man different? Didn't a man have a choice? How much did he know about his father, really?

"Hey, Dad."

"Yes, Jerry?"

"Nothing."

What could he ask him without sounding crazy? And he doubted whether his father would level with him, anyway. Jerry recalled an incident that had taken place years ago when his father worked in a neighborhood pharmacy, the kind of place where customers came to consult the druggist as if he possessed a doctor's certificate. Jerry had been hanging around the store one afternoon when an old man entered, bent and gnarled with age. He had a pain in his right side. What should I do, Mister Druggist? What do you think it is? Look, press here, Mister Druggist, do you feel the swelling there? Is there a medicine to cure me? His father had been patient with the old man, listening sympathetically, nodding, stroking his cheek as if he were preparing a diagnosis. He finally convinced the old man to go see a doctor. But for a moment there, Jerry had seen his father acting the part of a physician—wise and professional and compassionate. A regular bedside manner, even there in a drugstore. After the old man's departure, Jerry had asked, "Hey, Dad, did you ever want to be a doctor?" His father glanced up quickly and hesitated, taken by surprise. "No, of course not," he said. But Jerry had caught something in his manner, in his tone of voice, that ran counter to his answer. When Jerry tried to pursue the subject, his father suddenly became very busy with prescriptions and stuff. And he never brought up the subject again.

Now, seeing his father presiding in the kitchen, getting supper, for crying out loud—such a far cry from being a doctor—and his wife dead and his only son full of doubts about him, his life so pale and gray, Jerry was plunged into sadness. The stove signaled— casserole ready.

Later, preparing for bed and sleep, Jerry looked at himself in the mirror, saw himself as that guy on the

Common must have seen him the other day: Square Boy. Just as he had superimposed his mother's image on his father's face, now he could see his father's face reflected in his own features. He turned away. He didn't want to be a mirror of his father. The thought made him cringe. I want to do something, be somebody. But what? But what?

Football. He'd make the team. That was something. Or was it, really?

For no reason at all, he thought of Gregory Bailey.

Chapter 10

Later, Archie had to concede that Brother Leon had dramatized the sale too vividly and therefore put himself and The Vigils and the entire school on the spot.

To begin with, he called a special assembly at chapel. Following prayers and a lot of other religious hoopla, he started talking about all that school spirit crap. But with a difference this time. Standing at the pulpit, he gave the signal to a few of his stooges to bring in ten big cardboard posters which listed in alphabetical order every student in school. A series of blank rectangles had been drawn beside each name which, Leon explained, would be filled in as each student sold his quota of chocolates.

The student body watched with glee as Leon's stooges tried to scotch-tape the posters to the wall at the rear of the stage. The posters kept slipping to the floor, resisting the tape. The walls were made of concrete blocks, and tacks couldn't be used, of course. Hoots filled the air. Brother Leon looked annoyed, which increased the hoots and catcalls. There was nothing more beautiful in the world than the sight of a teacher getting upset. Finally, the posters were secured and Brother Leon took charge.

Archie had to admit that the Brother turned in one of his great performances. Academy Award caliber. He poured it on like Niagara—school spirit, the traditional sale that had never failed, the Headmaster lying sick in the hospital, the brotherhood of Trinity, the need for funds to keep this magnificent edifice of education operating on all gears. He recalled past triumphs, the trophies in the display case in the main corridor, the do-or-die determination that made Trinity a place of triumph through the years. Etc. Crap, of course, but effective when a master like Leon was at work, casting a spell with words and gestures.

"Yes," Brother Leon intoned, "the quota is doubled this year because we have more at stake than ever before." His voice an organ, filling the air. "Each boy must sell fifty boxes, but I know that each boy is willing to do his share. More than his share." He gestured toward the posters. "I promise you, gentlemen, that before this sale is ended each one of you will have the number 'fifty' inscribed in that final box, signifying that you have done your part for Trinity . . ."

There was a lot more but Archie tuned him out. Talk, talk, talk—that's all anybody ever heard in school. Archie squirmed uncomfortably in his seat, thinking of the Vigil meeting at which he had announced that Brother Leon had asked support for the sale and how he'd pledged the backing of The Vigils. Archie had been surprised at the ripple of doubt and skepticism from the members of The Vigils. "Christ, Archie," Carter had said, "we never get mixed up in this stuff." But Archie had overcome them as usual, pointing out that Leon's need for an endorsement from The Vigils was a symbol of how powerful the organization had become. And it was only a crappy chocolate sale. But now, listening to Leon sounding as if the school was embarking on the Crusades, for crying out loud, Archie was doubtful.

Looking at the posters and seeing his own name there, Archie plotted how his own fifty boxes would be sold. He wouldn't dream of selling the chocolates himself. He hadn't touched a box since his freshman days. Usually he found some willing kid who'd gladly sell Archie's quota along with his own, figuring it was something special to be singled out by the assigner of The Vigils. This year, he'd probably spread the burden around, picking out five guys, say, and have them sell only ten boxes each. It was better than sticking one kid with the entire quota, wasn't it?

Sitting back in comfort, Archie sighed now, contented, gratified by the heights his sense of fairness and compassion could reach.

Chapter 11

It was as if somebody had dropped The Bomb.

Brian Kelly started it all when he touched his chair. It collapsed.

Then, everything happened at once.

Albert LeBlanc brushed against a desk as he made his way down the aisle and it fell apart after trembling crazily for a moment. The impact sent out vibrations which shot down two other chairs and a desk.

John Lowe was about to sit down when he heard the noise of collapsing furniture. He turned and in doing so touched his own desk. The desk disintegrated before his astonished eyes. Leaping backward, he hit his chair. Nothing happened to his chair. But Henry Couture's desk behind it shivered violently and tumbled to the floor.

The racket was deafening.

"My God," Brother Eugene cried as he entered the classroom and beheld the bedlam. Desks and chairs were falling apart as if being demolished by mysterious unheard dynamite explosions.

Brother Eugene rushed to his desk, that haven of security behind which a teacher always found protection. At his touch, the desk swayed drunkenly, shifted gears into a lopsided position and—miracle of miracles—remained upright at that strange tipsy angle. But his chair collapsed.

Boys scrambled madly and merrily around the room. Once they realized what was happening they dashed around Room Nineteen testing all the desks and chairs, watching with glee as they fell apart, and toppling the stubborn pieces of furniture that refused to go down without help.

"Wow," somebody yelled.

"The Vigils," somebody else called out—giving credit where credit was due.

The destruction of Room Nineteen took exactly thirty-seven seconds. Archie timed it from the doorway. A sweetness gathered in his breast as he saw the room being turned into a shambles, a sweet moment of triumph that compensated for all the other lousy things, his terrible marks, the black box. Witnessing the pandemonium, he knew that this was one of his major triumphs, one of those long-shot assignments that paid off beautifully, certain to become legend. He could picture Trinity students of the future discussing in wonder the day Room Nineteen exploded. He found it hard to suppress a howl of delight as he surveyed the havoc—*I made this happen*—and saw Brother Eugene's trembling chin and horror-stricken expression.

Behind the brother, the huge blackboard suddenly tore loose from its moorings and slid majestically to the floor, like a final curtain dropping on the chaos.

"You!"

Archie heard the voice in all its fury at the same instant that he felt the hands spinning him around. He swiveled to encounter Brother Leon. Leon wasn't pale at this moment. Scarlet splotches glistened on his cheeks as if he had been made up for some grotesque stage show. A horror show maybe, because there was nothing funny about him at this moment.

"You!" Leon said again, a wicked whisper that spilled into Archie's face the foul aftertaste of Leon's breakfast—the smell of stale bacon and eggs. "You did this," Leon said, digging the fingernails of one hand into Archie's shoulder while pointing to the chaos of Room Nineteen with the other.

Curious students from other classes had now gathered around the two entrances to the room, drawn by the crash and clatter. Some of them regarded the rubble with awe. Others glanced curiously at Brother Leon and Archie. No matter where they looked, it was great—an interruption of school routine, a diversion in the deadly order of the day.

"Didn't I tell you I wanted everything to go smoothly? No incidents? No funny business?"

The worst part of Leon's fury was the way he whispered, this terrible tortured hissing from his mouth, giving his words a tone more deadly than a shout or a yell. At the same time his grip on Archie's shoulder got tighter and Archie winced with pain.

"I didn't do anything. I didn't promise anything," Archie said automatically. Always deny everything, never apologize, never admit anything.

Leon pushed Archie up against a wall as the boys began to fill the corridor, pouring into Room Nineteen to view the destruction, and milling around outside, talking and gesturing, shaking their heads in wonder—the legend had already begun.

"I'm in charge, don't you see? This entire school is now my responsibility. The chocolate sale is ready to start and you pull something like this." Leon released him without warning, and Archie hung there as if suspended in mid-air. He turned and saw some guys staring at Leon and him. Staring at him! Archie Costello humiliated by this snivelling bastard of a teacher. His sweet moment of triumph spoiled by this nut and his ridiculous chocolate sale!

He watched Leon storming away, pushing his way through the tumultuous corridor, disappearing into the swarming stream of boys. Archie massaged his shoulder, gingerly feeling the spot where Leon's fingernails had bitten deep. Then he thrust himself into the crowd, pushing aside the guys gathered near the doorway. He stood at the entrance, drinking in the beautiful debris of Room Nineteen—his masterpiece. He saw Brother Eugene still standing there in the midst of the shambles, tears actually running down his cheeks.

Beautiful, beautiful.

Screw Brother Leon.

Chapter 12

"Try it again," the coach bellowed, his voice hoarse. The danger point—his voice always got hoarse when he lost his patience, when he was in danger of blowing his top.

Jerry picked himself up. His mouth was dry and he tried to suck spit into it. His ribs hurt, his entire left side was on fire. He stalked back to his position behind Adamo who played center. The other guys were already lined up, tense, waiting, aware that the coach wasn't happy with them. Not happy? Hell, he was furious, disgusted. He had arranged this special practice giving his freshmen a chance to scrimmage against a few members of the varsity, to show off all he had taught them and they were doing lousy, rotten, terrible.

There was no huddle. The coach barked the number of the next play, a play designed to suck in Carter, the big beefy varsity guard who looked as if he could chew freshmen up and spit them out. But the coach had said, "We'll have some surprises for Carter." It was tradition at Trinity to toss star players against the freshmen and to build plays designed to stop the stars. This was the only reward the freshman team reaped because most of them were too young or too small to play varsity.

Jerry crouched behind Adamo. He was determined to make this play work. He knew that the previous play hadn't worked because his timing was off and because he hadn't seen Carter come crashing out of nowhere. He had expected Carter to blitz and instead the big guard had pulled back and skirted the line, annihilating Jerry from behind. What infuriated Jerry was that Carter toppled him gently, lowering him to the ground almost tenderly as if to prove his superiority. I don't have to murder you, kid, it's easy enough this way, Carter seemed to be saying. But this was the seventh consecutive play and the damage of being tackled play after play was taking its toll.

"All right, guys, this is it. Make or break."

"It's all over, fellas," Carter taunted.

Jerry called the signals, hoping his voice sounded confident. He didn't feel confident. And yet he hadn't given up hope. Every play was a new beginning and even though something always seemed to go wrong he felt that they were on the verge of clicking. He had confidence in guys like Goober and Adamo and Croteau. Sooner or later, they had to click, all the work had to pay off. That is, if the coach didn't cut them all off the squad first.

Jerry's hands were joined like a duck's bill waiting to swallow the ball. At his signal, Adamo slapped the ball into his palms and Jerry began to fade at the same instant, to the right, slanted, swift, his arm already coming up, ready to be cocked, ready for the pass. He saw Carter snaking through the line again, like some monstrous reptile in his helmet, but suddenly Carter became all arms and legs tossing and turning in the air, hit devastatingly low by Croteau. Carter collapsed on Croteau and both of them fell in a tangle of bodies. Jerry felt a sudden sense of freedom. He continued to fade, fade, easy, easy, stalling until he could spot The Goober, tall and rangy, downfield where he'd be waiting if he had managed to elude the safetyman. Suddenly Jerry spotted Goober's waving hand. Jerry avoided fingers that tore at his sleeve and he unloosed the ball. Someone brushed his hip but he shrugged off the blow. The pass was beautiful. He could tell it was beautiful, straight on target, even though he couldn't watch its progress, because he was dumped violently to the ground by Carter who had somehow recovered after being demolished. As he hit the ground, Jerry heard the yells and the cheers that told him The Goober had caught the pass and gone on to score.

"Good, good, good, good." The coach's voice, raucous in triumph.

Jerry struggled to his feet. Carter slapped him on the ass, signaling his approval.

The coach lumbered toward them, still scowling. But then he never smiled.

"Renault," the coach said, all hoarseness gone. "We just might make a quarterback out of you yet, you skinny little son of a bitch."

With the fellows standing all around him and his breath coming in gasps and Goober arriving with the ball, Jerry knew a moment of absolute bliss, absolute happiness.

There was a legend in the school that the coach hadn't accepted you as a player until he'd called you a son of a bitch.

The guys lined up again. Jerry was sweet poetry and music as he waited for the ball to be slapped into his hand.

When he returned to the school after practice, he found a letter scotch-taped to the door of his locker. A summons from The Vigils. Subject: Assignment.

Chapter 13

"Adamo?"

"Yes."

"Beauvais?"

"Yes."

"Crane?"

"Yo." Crane, the comedian. Never a straight answer.

"Caroni?"

"Yes."

Everyone could see that Brother Leon was enjoying himself. This is what he liked—to be in command and everything going smoothly, the students responding to their names smartly, accepting the chocolates, showing school spirit. The Goober was depressed, thinking about school spirit. Ever since Room Nineteen had collapsed, he had lived in a state of mild shock. He awoke each morning depressed, knowing even before he opened his eyes that something was wrong, something had gone askew in his life. And then he'd remember: Room Nineteen. The first day or two had been kind of exciting. Word had gotten around that the destruction of Room Nineteen was the result of his assignment by The Vigils. Although no one mentioned the subject to him, he found himself a kind of underground hero. Even the seniors looked at him with awe and respect. Guys patted him on the ass when he passed by, an old Trinity mark of distinction. But as the days went on, an uneasiness stole across the campus. There were rumors. The place was always filled with rumors but this time they grew out of the Room Nineteen incident. The chocolate sale was postponed for a week and Brother Leon, speaking at chapel, gave a weak explanation. The Head was hospitalized, there was a lot of paperwork involved, etc. etc. There were also rumors that Leon was carrying on a quiet investigation of Room Nineteen. Poor Brother Eugene had not been seen since that devastating morning. He'd had a nervous breakdown, someone said. Others reported that there had been a death in his family and he'd been called away. Anyway, it all heaped itself upon The Goober and he found it hard to sleep at night. Despite the adulation of the guys at school, he felt as if there was some kind of distance between him and the fellows. They admired him, sure, but didn't want to get too close in case something backfired. One afternoon, he'd met Archie Costello in the corridor and Archie had pulled him aside. "If they call you in for questioning, you know nothing," Archie said. Goober had no way of knowing this was the kind of thing Archie loved to do—intimidate someone, get him worrying. Since then, The Goober had walked around in a state of apprehension, expecting to see his name on a Wanted sign on the bulletin board, for crying out loud. He didn't want the adulation of the fellows anymore—he simply wanted to be The Goober, to play football and to run in the morning. He dreaded a summons from Brother Leon, wondering if he could stand up under questioning, whether he could look into those moist eyes of Brother Leon's and actually lie to him.

"Goubert?"

He realized that Brother Leon had been calling his name, two or three times.

"Yes," The Goober replied.

Brother Leon paused, looking at him questioningly. The Goober shriveled.

"You don't seem to be entirely with us today, Goubert," Leon said. "At least, not in spirit."

"I'm sorry, Brother Leon."

"Speaking of spirit, Goubert, you realize, don't you, how this chocolate sale goes beyond a mere sale or routine project, don't you?"

"Yes, Brother Leon." Was Leon baiting him?

"The most beautiful part of the sale, Goubert, is that it's a project completely by students. The students sell the chocolates. The school merely administers the project. It's *your* sale, *your* project."

Bullshit, someone whispered, out of Leon's hearing.

"Yes, Brother Leon," Goober said, relieved, realizing that the teacher was too much involved with the chocolates to be assessing Goober's innocence or guilt.

"Then you accept the fifty boxes?"

"Yes," Goober said with eagerness. Fifty boxes was a lot of chocolates but he was glad to say yes and get out of the spotlight.

Leon's hand moved ceremoniously as he wrote down Goober's name.

"Hartnett?"

"Yes."

"Johnson?"

"Why not?"

Leon accepted this small hint of mockery from Johnson because he was in such a good mood. The Goober wondered whether he himself would ever be in a good mood again. And he was puzzled. Why should he be feeling so lousy about Room Nineteen? Was it the destruction? Actually, the desks and chairs had been put back together again in one day. Leon had thought he was inflicting punishment on the fellows selected to do the job but the discipline backfired. Each screw, each piece of furniture was a reminder of that marvelous event. Fellows even volunteered for the job. Then, why this terrible guilt? Because of Brother Eugene? Probably. Whenever Goober walked by Room Nineteen now, he couldn't resist glancing in.

The room would never be the same again, of course. The furniture creaked weirdly, as if it would collapse again without warning. The various teachers who used the room were uneasy—you could tell they were apprehensive. Once in a while, some guy would drop a book just to see the teacher flinch or leap in panic.

Immersed in his thoughts, The Goober didn't realize that a terrible silence had enveloped the classroom. But he became aware of the stillness when he glanced up to see Brother Leon's face, paler now than ever, and the eyes glistening like sun-splashed pools.

"Renault?"

The silence continued.

The Goober glanced toward Jerry three desks away. Jerry sat stiffly, elbows resting on the desk, staring straight ahead, as if he were in a trance.

"You *are* here, aren't you, Renault?" Leon asked, trying to turn the moment into a joke. But his effort had the opposite effect. No one laughed.

"Last call, Renault."

"No," Jerry said.

The Goober wasn't sure he'd heard correctly. Jerry had spoken so quietly, barely moving his lips, that his answer had been indistinct even in that utter quiet.

"What?" From Leon.

"No."

Confusion now. Someone laughed. A classroom

joke was always appreciated, anything to fracture the dullness of routine.

"Did you say *no*, Renault?" Brother Leon asked, his voice testy.

"Yes."

"Yes, what?"

The exchange delighted the classroom. A giggle from somewhere and then a snort, followed by the strange mood that took hold of a classroom when the unusual occurred, the way students sensed a difference in the climate, an alteration of atmosphere, like the seasons changing.

"Let me get this straight, Renault," Brother Leon said and his voice brought the room under his command again. "I called your name. Your response could have been either *yes* or *no*. *Yes* means that like every other student in this school you agree to sell a certain amount of chocolates, in this case fifty boxes. *No*—and let me point out that the sale is strictly voluntary, Trinity forces no one to participate against his wishes, this is the great glory of Trinity—*no* means you don't wish to sell the chocolates, that you refuse to participate. Now, what is your answer? Yes or no?"

"No."

The Goober stared at Jerry in disbelief. Was this Jerry Renault who always looked a little worried, a little unsure of himself even after completing a beautiful pass, who always seemed kind of bewildered—was this him actually defying Brother Leon? Not only Brother Leon but a Trinity tradition? Then, looking at Leon, Goober saw the teacher as if in technicolor, blood beating in his cheeks, his moist eyes like specimens in laboratory test tubes. Finally, Brother Leon inclined his head, the pencil moving in his hand as he made some kind of horrible mark beside Jerry's name.

The silence in the class was the kind Goober had never heard before. Stunned, eerie, suffocating.

"Santucci?" Leon called out, his voice strangled but struggling to be normal.

"Yes."

Leon looked up, smiling at Santucci, blinking away the flush on his cheeks, a smile like the kind an undertaker fixes on the face of a corpse.

"Tessier?"

"Yes."

"Williams?"

"Yes."

Williams was the last. There was no one in this class with a name beginning with X, Y, or Z. Williams' *yes* lingered on the air. No one seemed to be looking at anyone else.

"You may pick up your chocolates in the gym, gentlemen," Brother Leon said, his eyes bright—wet bright. "Those of you who are true sons of Trinity, that is. I pity anyone who is not." That terrible smile remained on his face. "Class dismissed," Leon called although the bell had not sounded.

Chapter 14

Let's see, he knew he could count on his Aunt Agnes and Mike Terasigni whose lawn he cut every week in the summer, and Father O'Toole at the rectory (although his mother would massacre him if she knew he had Father O'Toole on the list) and Mr. and Mrs. Thornton who weren't Catholic but always willing to help a good cause, and, of course, Mrs. Mitchell the widow whose errands he did every Saturday morning and Henry Babineau the bachelor with his awful breath that almost knocked you down when you opened the door but who was pointed out by all the mothers in the neighborhood as the kindest, most gentlest of men . . .

John Sulkey liked to make out the lists whenever there was a sale at the school. Last year, as a junior, he had won first prize for selling the most chances in a school raffle—one hundred and twenty-five books, twelve tickets in each book—and received a special pin at the Awards Assembly at the end of the school year. The only honor he had ever won—purple and gold (the school colors), shaped like a triangle, symbolizing the trinity. His parents had beamed with pride. He was lousy at sports and a squeaker at studies—just barely squeaking by—but, like his mother said, you did your best and God took care of the rest. Of course, it took planning. That's why John made out his lists ahead of time. Sometimes he even visited his regular customers before a sale began to let them know what was coming. He liked nothing better than getting out there on the street and ringing the doorbells and seeing the money pile up, money he would turn in the next day at roll call, and how the Brother in the homeroom would smile down on him. He remembered with a glow when he went up to the stage for his award last year and how the Headmaster had talked about Service To The School, and how "John Sulkey exemplified these special attributes" (the exact words which still echoed in John's mind, especially when he saw those undistinguished rows of C's and D's on his report card every term). Anyway. Another sale. Chocolates. Double last year's price but John was confident. Brother Leon had promised to put up a special honor roll on the bulletin board in the main first-floor corridor for those who made their quota or exceeded it. A quota of fifty boxes. Higher than ever before, which made John happy. It would be harder for the other guys to meet the quota—already they were groaning and moaning—but John was supremely confident. In fact, when Brother Leon had told them about the special honor roll, John Sulkey could have sworn he was looking directly at him—as if Brother Leon was counting personally on him to set a good example.

So, let's see, the new housing development on Maple Terrace. Maybe he should make a special campaign in that neighborhood this year. There were nine or ten new homes there. But first of all, the old faithfuls, the people who had become regular customers: Mrs. Swanson who sometimes smelled of liquor but was always eager to buy anything although she kept him talking too long, rambling on about people John Sulkey didn't even know; and good old reliable Uncle Louie who was always simonizing his car although simonizing cars seemed part of the Dark Ages these days; and then the Capolettis at the end of the street who always invited him in for something to eat, cold pizza that John wasn't exactly crazy about and the smell of garlic that almost knocked you down but you had to make sacrifices, big and small, for the sake of Service To The School . . .

"Adamo?"
"Four."
"Beauvais?"
"One."
Brother Leon paused and looked up.
"Beauvais, Beauvais. You can do better than that. Only one? Why, last year you set a record for the number of boxes sold in a week."
"I'm a slow starter," Beauvais said. He was a good-natured kid, not exactly a whiz in his studies but likeable, without an enemy in the world. "Check me next week," he said.
The class laughed and the Brother joined in the laughter. The Goober laughed, too, grateful for the small relaxation of tension. He found that in recent days the kids in class had a tendency to laugh at things that weren't really funny, simply because they seemed to be looking for something to divert them for a few moments, to prolong the roll call, prolong it until the R's were reached. Everyone knew what would happen when Renault's name came up. It was as if by laughing they could ignore the situation.
"Fontaine?"
"Ten!"
A burst of applause led by Brother Leon himself.
"Wonderful, Fontaine. True spirit, a wonderful display of spirit."
Goober found it hard to resist looking at Jerry. His friend sat stiff and tense, his knuckles white. This was the fourth day of the sale and Jerry still called out *no* in the morning, staring straight ahead, rigid,

determined. Forgetting his own troubles for a moment, Goober had tried approaching Jerry as they left the field after practice the day before. But Jerry pulled away. "Let me alone, Goob," he said. "I know what you want to ask—but don't."

"Parmentier?"

"Six."

And then the gathering of tension. Jerry was next. Goober heard a weird sound, almost as if the class had sucked in its breath all at once.

"Renault?"

"No."

Pause. You'd think Brother Leon would have gotten used to the situation by now, that he'd skip quickly over Renault's name. But each day, the teacher's voice sang out with hope and each day the negative response was given.

"Santucci?"

"Three."

The Goober exhaled. So did the rest of the class. Strictly by accident, Goober happened to look up as Brother Leon marked down Santucci's report. He saw Leon's hand trembling. He had a terrible feeling of doom about to descend on all of them.

The short fat legs of Tubs Casper carried him through the neighborhood in what for him was record time. He'd have made better time if one of his bicycle tires wasn't flat, not only flat but definitely beyond repair and he didn't have money to buy a new tire. In fact, it was a desperate need for money that sent Tubs scurrying around town like a madman, from one house to another, lugging the chocolates, knocking at doors and ringing doorbells. He also had to do it furtively, afraid that his father or mother might see him. Small chance his father would come across him—he was at work at the plastic shop. But his mother was another thing altogether. She was a nut about the car, like his father said, and couldn't bear to stay home and was always driving around.

Tubs' left arm began to ache from the weight of the chocolates and he shifted his burden to his other arm, taking a moment to pat the reassuring bulge of his wallet. He had already sold three boxes—six dollars—but that wasn't enough, of course. He was still desperate. He needed a hell of a lot more by tonight and nobody but nobody had bought any chocolates at the last six houses he'd visited. He had saved every cent he could from his allowance and had even sneaked a folded and greasy dollar bill from his father's pocket last night when he arrived home, half-drunk and wobbly. He hated doing that—stealing from his own father. He vowed to return the money to him as soon as possible. When would that be? Tubs didn't know. Money, money, money had become the constant need of his life, money and his love for Rita. His allowance barely made it possible for him to take her to the movies and for a coke afterward. Two-fifty each for the movies, fifty cents for two cokes. And his parents hated her for some reason. He had to sneak out to meet her. He had to make phone calls from Ossie Baker's house. She's too old for you, his mother said, when actually Tubs himself was six months older. All right, she *looks* old, his mother said. What his mother should have said was, she looks beautiful. She was so beautiful that she made Tubs all shaky inside, like an earthquake going on. At night in bed, he could have one without even touching himself, just thinking of her. And now her birthday was tomorrow and he had to buy her the present she wanted, the bracelet she'd seen in the window of Black's downtown, that terrible and beautiful bracelet all sparkles and radiance, terrible because of the price tag: $18.95 plus tax. *"Hon,"*—she never called him Tubs—"that's what I want most in all the world." Jesus—$18.95 plus the 3 per cent sales tax which Tubs figured out would make a grand total of $19.52, the sales tax amounting to fifty-seven cents. He knew that he didn't have to buy her the bracelet.

She was a sweet girl who loved him for himself alone. She walked along the sidewalk with him, her breast brushing his arm, setting him on fire. The first time she rubbed against him he thought it was an accident and he pulled away, apologetic, leaving a space between them. Then she brushed against him again—that was the night he'd bought her the earrings—and he knew it wasn't an accident. He'd felt himself hardening and was suddenly ashamed and embarrassed and deliriously happy all at the same time. Him—Tubs Casper, forty pounds overweight which his father never let him forget. Him—with this beautiful girl's breast pushed against him, not beautiful the way his mother thought a girl was beautiful but beautiful in a ripe wild way, faded blue jeans hugging her hips, those beautiful breasts bouncing under her jersey. She was only fourteen and he was barely fifteen but they were in love, love dammit, and it was only money that kept them apart, money to take the bus to her house because she lived on the other side of town and they'd made plans to meet tomorrow, her birthday, at Monument Park, a picnic sort of, she'd bring the sandwiches and he'd bring the bracelet—he knew the delights that awaited him but he also knew deep down inside that the bracelet was more important than anything else . . .

All of which rushed him along now, out of breath and out of shape, trying to raise money that he knew dimly would lead him eventually only to trouble.

Where would he raise enough money to pay it all back when the returns were due at school? But what the hell—he'd worry about it later. Right now he needed to raise the money and Rita loved him—tomorrow she'd probably let him get under her sweater.

He rang the doorbell of a rich-looking house on Sterns Avenue and prepared his most innocent and sweetest smile for whoever opened the door.

The woman's hair was damp and askew, and a little kid, maybe two or three years old, was tugging at her skirt. "Chocolates?" she asked, laughing bitterly as if Paul Consalvo had suggested the most absurd thing in the world. "You want me to buy chocolates?"

The baby, wearing a soggy-looking droopy diaper, was calling, "Mommy . . . mommy . . ." And another kid was howling somewhere in the apartment.

"It's for a good cause," Paul said. "Trinity School!"

Paul's nose wrinkled at the smell of pee.

"Jesus," the woman said. "Chocolates!"

"Mommee . . . mommee . . ." the kid squalled.

Paul felt sorry for older people, stuck in their houses and tenements with kids to take care of and housework to do. He thought of his own parents and their useless lives—his father collapsing into his nap every night after supper and his mother looking tired and dragged-out all the time. What the hell were they living for? He couldn't wait to get out of the house. "Where're you going all the time?" his mother asked as he fled the place. How could he tell her that he hated the house, that his mother and father were dead and didn't know it, that if it wasn't for television the place would be like a tomb. He couldn't say that because he really loved them and if the house caught fire in the middle of the night he'd rescue them, he'd be willing to sacrifice his own life for them. But, jeez, it was so boring, so deadly at home—what did they have to live for? They were too old for sex even, although Paul turned away from the thought. He couldn't believe that his mother and father ever actually . . .

"Sorry," the woman said, shutting the door in his face, still shaking her head in wonder at his sales pitch.

Paul stood in the doorway, wondering what to do. He'd had rotten luck this afternoon, hadn't sold a single box. He hated selling them anyway, although it gave him an excuse to get out of the house. But he couldn't really put his heart in it. He was just going through the motions.

Outside the apartment house, Paul considered his choices: pressing on with the sale despite his luck today or going home. He crossed the street and rang the doorbell of another apartment building. In an apartment house, you could knock off five or six families at one time even though the places all seemed to smell of pee.

Brother Leon had "volunteered" Brian Cochran for the position of Treasurer of the Chocolate Sale. Which meant that he'd looked around the classroom, pinned those watery eyes on Brian, pointed his finger and, *voilà*, as Brother Aimé said in French class, Brian was treasurer. He hated the job because he lived in fear of Brother Leon. You never knew about Leon. Brian was a senior and he'd had Leon as either a classroom teacher or as homeroom supervisor for four years and he was still uncomfortable in his presence. The teacher was unpredictable and yet predictable at the same time, which reasoning confused Brian because he wasn't exactly a hotshot in the psychology department. It was this: you knew that Leon would always do the unexpected—wasn't that being both predictable and unpredictable? He loved to toss surprise exams at a class—and he also could suddenly be the nice guy, not giving a test for weeks or giving a test and then throwing away the results. Or concocting a pass-fail test—he was famous for that type—where he threaded together questions that could throw a guy for a loss, with what seemed like a million possible answers. He was also quite a man with the pointer although he usually confined that kind of stuff to freshmen. If he ever pulled the pointer antics with, say, somebody like Carter, there'd be hell to pay. But not everybody was John Carter, president of The Vigils, All-Star Guard on the football team, and president of the Boxing Club. How Brian Cochran would love to be like John Carter, with muscles instead of glasses, quick with boxing gloves instead of figures.

Speaking of figures, Brian Cochran began double-checking the sales totals. As usual, there was a discrepancy between the amount of chocolates reported as sold and the actual money received. The guys were notorious for holding back some of the money until the last minute. Ordinarily, nobody got excited about it—it was human nature. A lot of the guys sold chocolates, spent the money on a big date or a big night, and then put in the money when they got their allowance or their pay at their part-time jobs. But this year, Brother Leon acted as if every dollar was a matter of life and death. In fact, he was driving Brian Cochran up a wall.

The job of treasurer called for Brian to check every homeroom at the end of the day and write down the returns the boys had reported. How many boxes sold. How much money turned in. Brian then went to

Brother Leon's office and totaled all the figures. Then Brother Leon would come along and check Brian's report. Simple, right? Wrong. The way Brother Leon was carrying on this year made every day's report seem like a major headline event. Brian had never seen the Brother so edgy, so nervous. At first he'd gotten a kick out of the teacher's apprehension, the way the sweat poured off him like he had a special pump inside producing all that perspiration. When he came into the office and took off the black suit coat he was required to wear in the classroom during all seasons, sweat stains darkened his armpits, and he smelled as if he'd just gone ten rounds in the ring. He fidgeted and fussed around, double-checking Brian's figures, chewing on a pencil, pacing the floor.

Today, Brian was more puzzled than ever. Leon had passed around a report to all the homerooms listing total sales thus far at 4,582. Which was wrong. The kids had sold exactly 3,961 boxes and had made returns on 2,871. Sales were definitely lagging behind last year and so was the money. He couldn't understand why Leon had issued a false report. Did he think he could hype them up that way?

Brian shrugged, tabulating his own totals once more to be sure that Brother Leon wouldn't blame him for any discrepancies. He'd hate to have Leon for an enemy, which is one reason he'd accepted the job of treasurer without making waves. Brian was a member of Leon's algebra class and he didn't want to take any chances with extra homework or sudden unexplained *F*'s on exams.

Looking at the summary once again, Brian saw the zero next to the name of Jerome Renault. He chuckled. That was the freshman who refused to sell any chocolates. Brian shook his head—who'd want to buck the system? Hell, who'd want to buck Brother Leon? The kid must be some kind of madman.

"LeBlanc?"

"Six."

"Malloran?"

"Three."

The pause. The intake of breath. It had gotten to be a game now—this roll call, this fascinating moment in Brother Leon's homeroom. Even Goober couldn't help but get caught up in the tension although the entire situation made him slightly sick to his stomach. Goober was a peaceful figure. He hated strain, contention. Peace, let's have peace. But there was no peace in Brother Leon's room in the morning as he called the roll of chocolate sales. He stood tense at the desk, those watery eyes blinking in the morning light, while Jerry Renault sat as usual at his desk, without emotion, frigid, elbows resting on the surface of the desk.

"Parmentier?"

"Two."

Now—

"Renault."

Inhale.

"No."

Exhale.

The color spreading on Leon's face, like his veins had turned into scarlet neon signs.

"Santucci?"

"Two."

The Goober couldn't wait for the bell to ring.

Chapter 15

"Hey Archie," Emile Janza called.

"Yes, Emile."

"You still got the picture?"

"What picture?" Suppressing a smile.

"You know what picture."

"Oh, *that* picture. Yes, Emile, I still have it."

"I don't suppose it's for sale, Archie."

"Not for sale, Emile. What would you want with that picture, anyway? To tell the truth, Emile, it's not the greatest picture ever taken of you. I mean, you're not even smiling or anything. There's this funny look on your face. But you're not smiling, Emile."

There was a funny look on Emile Janza's face right at this moment and he wasn't smiling now either. Anyone else but Archie would have been intimidated by that look.

"Where do you keep the picture, Archie?"

"It's safe, Emile. Very safe."

"That's good."

Archie wondered, should I tell him the truth about the picture? He knew that Emile Janza could be a dangerous enemy. On the other hand, the photograph also could be used as a weapon.

"Tell you what, Emile," Archie said. "Someday you might be able to get the photograph all for yourself."

Janza flipped his cigarette against a tree and watched the butt ricochet into the gutter. He withdrew a package from his pocket, discovered it was empty and tossed it away, watching the breeze move it along on the sidewalk. Emile Janza didn't care about keeping America beautiful.

"How can I get the photograph, Archie?"

"Well, you won't have to buy it, Emile."

"You mean you'd give it to me? There must be a catch, Archie."

"There is, Emile. But nothing you can't handle when the time comes."

"You let me know when the time comes. Okay, Archie?" Emile asked, giggling his foolish giggle.

"You'll be the first to know," Archie said.

The tone of their conversation had been light, bantering, but Archie knew that Emile was deadly serious underneath. Archie also knew that Janza would be willing to practically murder him in his sleep to get his hot hands on the picture. And the terrible irony—there was no picture after all. Archie had merely taken advantage of a ridiculous situation. What happened was this: Archie had cut a class and glided through the corridor, evading the brothers. Moving past an open locker, he'd spotted a camera dangling from one of the coat hooks. Automatically, Archie had taken the camera. He wasn't a thief, of course. He figured he'd merely abandon it somewhere so that the owner, whoever he was, would have to chase around the school looking for it. Stepping into the men's room to grab a quick smoke, Archie had pulled open the door to one of the stalls and confronted Janza sitting there, pants dropping on the floor, one hand furiously at work between his legs. Archie lifted the camera and pretended to take a picture, yelling "Hold it."

"Beautiful," Archie had called.

Janza had been too shocked and surprised to react quickly. By the time he had recovered, Archie was at the doorway, poised to flee if Janza made a move.

"Better hand over that camera," Janza called.

"If you're going to jack off in a toilet, at least lock your door," Archie taunted.

"The lock's broken," Emile replied. "All the locks are broken."

"Well, don't worry, Emile. Your secret is safe with me."

Now Janza turned from Archie and spotted a freshman hurrying across the street, evidently worried because he was afraid of being late for classes. It took a year or two to develop the timing that allowed you to linger until the last possible moment at the doorway.

"Hey, freshman," Janza called.

The kid looked up, panic-stricken, when he saw Janza.

"Afraid you're going to be late?"

The kid gulped, nodding his head.

"Have no fear, freshman."

The final whistle blew. Exactly forty-five seconds to make it to homerooms.

"I'm all out of cigarettes," Emile declared, patting his pockets.

Archie smiled, knowing what Janza planned. Janza considered himself a candidate for The Vigils and he was always trying to impress Archie.

"What I'd like, kid, is for you to run over to Baker's and buy me a pack of cigarettes."

"I haven't got any money," the boy protested. "And I'll be late for school."

"That's life, kid. That's the way it goes. Heads I win, tails you lose. If you haven't got the money, steal the smokes. Or borrow the money. Just meet me at lunch with the cigarettes. Any brand. Emile Janza's not fussy." Tossing in his name so that the kid would know who he was dealing with in the event he hadn't been tipped off about Emile Janza.

Archie lingered, knowing he was flirting with a tardy rap. But he was fascinated by Janza, crude and gross as he was. The world was made up of two kinds of people—those who were victims and those who victimized. There was no doubt about Janza's category. No doubt about himself, either. And no doubt about the kid, taking off down the hill, tears spilling onto his cheeks as he turned away.

"He's got the money, Archie," Emile said. "Don't you figure he's got the money and was lying through his teeth?"

"I'll bet you also kick old ladies down the stairs and trip cripples on the street," Archie said.

Janza giggled.

The giggle chilled Archie who himself was considered capable of hurting little old ladies and tripping cripples.

Chapter 16

"Such a terrible mark, Caroni."

"I know, I know."

"And you are usually such a splendid scholar."

"Thank you, Brother Leon."

"How are your other marks?"

"Fine, Brother, fine. In fact, I thought . . . I mean, I was aiming for high honors this term. But now, this *F* . . ."

"I know," the teacher said, shaking his head sorrowfully, in commiseration.

Caroni was confused. He had never received an *F* before in his life. In fact, he had seldom received a mark lower than an *A*. In the seventh and eighth grades at St. Jude's, he had received straight *A*'s for two years except for a *B*-plus one term. He had scored so high on the Trinity entrance exam that he had been awarded one of the rare Trinity scholarships—one hundred dollars contributed toward his tuition, and his picture in the paper. And then this terrible *F*, a routine test turning into a nightmare.

"The *F* surprised me as well," Brother Leon said. "Because you are such an excellent student, David."

Caroni looked up in sudden wonder and hope. Brother Leon seldom called a student by his first name. He always kept a distance between himself and his pupils. "There is an invisible line between teacher and student," he always said, "and it must not be crossed." But, now, hearing him pronounce "David" in such friendly fashion and with such gentleness and understanding, Caroni allowed himself to hope—but for what? Had the *F* been a mistake, after all?

"This was a difficult test for several reasons," the teacher went on. "One of those exams where the wrong, subtle interpretation of the facts made the difference between pass and fail. In fact, that was it exactly—a pass-fail test. And when I read your answer, David, for a moment I thought it was possible that you had passed. In many respects you were correct in your assertions. But, on the other hand . . ." His voice trailed away, he seemed deep in thought, troubled.

Caroni waited. A horn blew outside—the school bus lumbering away. He thought of his father and mother and what they would do when they learned of the *F*. It would drag down his average—it was almost impossible to overcome an *F* no matter how many other *A*'s he managed to make.

"One thing students don't always realize, David," Brother Leon went on, speaking softly, intimately, as if there were no one in the world except them, as if he had never talked to anyone in the world the way he was talking to David at this moment, "one thing they don't grasp is that teachers are human too. Human like other people." Brother Leon smiled as if he had made a joke. Caroni allowed himself a small smile, unsure of himself, not wanting to do the wrong thing. The classroom was suddenly warm, it seemed crowded although there were just the two of them there. "Yes, yes, we are all too human. We have our good days and our bad days. We get tired. Our judgment sometimes becomes impaired. We sometimes—as the boys say—goof. It's possible even for us to make mistakes correcting papers, especially when the answers are not cut and dried, not one thing or another, not all black nor all white . . ."

Caroni was all ears now, alert—what was Brother Leon driving at? He looked sharply at Brother Leon.

The teacher looked as he always did—the moist eyes that reminded Caroni of boiled onions, the pale damp skin, and the cool talk, always under control. He held a piece of white chalk in his hand like a cigarette. Or maybe like a miniature pointer.

"Did you ever hear a teacher admit that it's possible for him to make a mistake, David? Ever hear that before?" Brother Leon asked, laughing.

"Like an umpire saying he made the wrong call," Caroni said, joining in the teacher's little joke. But why the joke? Why all this talk of mistakes?

"Yes, yes," Leon agreed. "No one is without error. And it's understandable. We all have our duties and we must discharge them. The Headmaster is still in the hospital and I take it as a privilege to act in his behalf. Besides this, there are the extracurricular activities. The chocolate sale, for instance . . ."

Brother Leon's grip was tight on the piece of chalk. Caroni noticed how his knuckles were almost as white as the chalk itself. He waited for the teacher to continue. But there was only silence. Caroni watched the chalk in Brother Leon's hands, the way the teacher pressed it, rolled it, his fingers like the legs of pale spiders with a victim in their clutch.

"But it's all rewarding," Leon went on. How was it that his voice was so cool when the hand holding the chalk was so tense, the veins sticking out, as if threatening to burst through the flesh?

"Rewarding?" Caroni had lost the thread of Brother Leon's thought.

"The chocolate sale," Leon said.

And the chalk split in his hand.

"For instance," Leon said, dropping the pieces and opening the ledger that was so familiar to everyone at Trinity, the ledger in which the daily sales were recorded. "Let me see—you have done fine in the sale,

David. Eighteen boxes sold. Fine. Fine. Not only are you an excellent scholar but you possess school spirit."

Caroni blushed with pleasure—it was impossible for him to resist a compliment, even when he was all mixed up as he certainly was at the moment. All this talk of exams and teachers getting tired and making mistakes and now the chocolate sale . . . and the two pieces of broken chalk abandoned on the desk, like white bones, dead men's bones.

"If everyone did his part like you, David, the sale would be an instant success. Of course, not everyone has your spirit, David . . ."

Caroni wasn't sure what tipped him off. Maybe the way Brother Leon paused at this point. Maybe the entire conversation, all of it off-key somehow. Or maybe the chalk in Brother Leon's hands, the way he had snapped it in two while his voice remained cool and easy—which was the phony thing: the hand holding the chalk, all tense and nervous, or the cool, easy voice?

"Take Renault, for instance," Brother Leon continued. "Funny thing about him, isn't it?"

And Caroni knew. He found himself staring into the moist watchful eyes of the teacher and in a blinding flash he knew what this was all about, what was happening, what Brother Leon was doing, the reason for this little conversation after school. A headache began to assert itself above his right eye, the pain digging into his flesh—migraine. His stomach lurched sickeningly. Were teachers like everyone else, then? Were teachers as corrupt as the villains you read about in books or saw in movies and television? He'd always worshiped his teachers, had thought of becoming a teacher himself someday if he could overcome his shyness. But now—this. The pain grew in intensity, throbbing in his forehead.

"Actually, I feel badly for Renault," Brother Leon was saying. "He must be a very troubled boy to act this way."

"I guess so," Caroni said, stalling, uncertain of himself and yet knowing really what Brother Leon wanted. He had seen Brother Leon every day in the classroom calling out the names and had watched him recoil as if from a blow when Jerry Renault continued to refuse the chocolates. It had become a kind of joke among the fellows. Actually, Caroni had felt badly for Jerry Renault. He knew that no kid was a match for Brother Leon. But now he realized that Brother Leon had been the victim. He must have been climbing the walls all this time, David thought.

"Well, David."

And the echo of his name here in the classroom startled him. He wondered if he still had aspirins left in his locker. Forget the aspirins, forget the headache. He knew now what the score was, what Leon was waiting to hear. Yet, could he be sure?

"Speaking of Jerry Renault . . ." Caroni said—a safe beginning, a statement he could draw back from, depending on Brother Leon's reaction.

"Yes?"

The hand had picked up one of the pieces of chalk again, and that "Yes?" had been too quick, too sudden to allow any doubt. Caroni found himself hung up between choices and the headache didn't help matters. Could he erase that *F* by telling Brother Leon simply what he wanted to hear? What was so terrible about that? On the other hand, an *F* could ruin him. And how about all the other *F*'s it was possible that Leon could give him in the future?

"Funny thing about Jerry Renault," Caroni heard

himself saying. And then instinct caused him to add, "But I'm sure you know what it's all about, Brother Leon. The Vigils. The assignment . . ."

"Of course, of course," Leon said, sitting back, letting the chalk fall gently from his hand.

"It's a Vigil stunt. He's supposed to refuse to sell chocolates for ten days—ten school days—and then accept them. Boy, those Vigils, they're really something, aren't they?" His head was killing him and his stomach was a sea of nausea.

"Boys will be boys," Leon was saying, nodding his head, his voice a whisper—it was hard to tell whether he was surprised or relieved. "Knowing Trinity's spirit, it was obvious, of course. Poor Renault. You remember, Caroni, that I said he must be troubled. Terrible, to force a boy into that kind of situation, against his will. But it's all over then, isn't it? The ten days—why they're up, let's see, tomorrow." He was smiling now, gayly, and talking as if the words themselves didn't matter but that it was important to talk, as if the words were safety valves. And then Caroni realized that Brother Leon had used his name but this time he hadn't said *David* . . .

"Well, I guess that's it then," Brother Leon said, rising, "I've detained you too long, Caroni."

"Brother Leon," Caroni said. He couldn't be dismissed at this point. "You said you wanted to discuss my mark . . ."

"Oh, yes, yes, that's right, my boy. That *F* of yours."

Caroni felt doom pressing upon him. But went on anyway. "You said teachers make mistakes, they get tired . . ."

Brother Leon was standing now. "Tell you what, Caroni. At the end of the term, when the marks close,

I'll review that particular test. Perhaps I'll be fresher then. Perhaps I'll see merit that wasn't apparent before . . ."

Now it was Caroni's turn to feel relief from the tension, although his headache still pounded and his stomach was still upset. Worse than that, however, he had allowed Brother Leon to blackmail him. If teachers did this kind of thing, what kind of world could it be?

"On the other hand, Caroni, perhaps the *F* will stand," Brother Leon said. "It depends . . ."

"I see, Brother Leon," Caroni said.

And he did see—that life was rotten, that there were no heroes, really, and that you couldn't trust anybody, not even yourself.

He had to get out of there as fast as possible, before he vomited all over Brother Leon's desk.

Chapter 17

"Adamo?"

"Three."

"Beauvais?"

"Five."

The Goober was impatient for the roll call to be over. Or, rather, for the roll call to reach Jerry Renault. Like everyone else, The Goober had finally learned that Jerry was carrying out a Vigil assignment—that's why he had refused to take the chocolates day after day, that's why he didn't want to talk about it with Goober. Now, Jerry could become himself again, human again. His football had suffered. "What the hell is the matter with you, Renault?" the coach asked in disgust yesterday, "do you want to play ball or not?" And Jerry had answered, "I'm playing ball." All the kids knew the double meaning his answer conveyed because it was public knowledge now. He and Goober had had only one brief conversation about the assignment—in fact, it wasn't really a conversation. Leaving football practice yesterday, Goober had whispered, "When does the assignment end?" And Jerry had said, "Tomorrow I take the chocolates."

"Hartnett?"

"One."

"You can do better than that, Hartnett," Leon said, but there was no anger, not even disappointment in his voice. Brother Leon was buoyant today and his mood had spread throughout the class. That's the way Leon's classes were—he set the mood and the temperature.

When Brother Leon was happy everybody was happy, when he was miserable everybody was miserable.

"Johnson?"

"Five."

"Good, good."

Killelea . . . LeBlanc . . . Malloran . . . the roll call went on, the voices shouting out their sales and the teacher checking the names off on the sheet. The names and the responses sounded almost like a song, a melody for a classroom, a tune for many voices. Then Brother Leon called out "Parmentier." And there was tension in the air. Parmentier could have called out any number and it wouldn't have mattered, it wouldn't have created any impact at all. Because the next name was Renault.

"Three," Parmentier called out.

"Right," Brother Leon answered, making the check against the name. Looking up, he called "Renault."

The pause. The damn pause.

"No!"

The Goober felt as if his eyes were the lens for a television camera in one of those documentaries. He swung around in Jerry's direction and saw his friend's face, white, mouth half-open, his arms dangling at his sides. And then he swiveled to look at Brother Leon and saw the shock on the teacher's face, his mouth forming an oval of astonishment. It seemed almost as if Jerry and the teacher were reflections in a mirror.

Finally Brother Leon looked down.

"Renault," he said again, his voice like a whip.

"No. I'm not going to sell the chocolates."

Cities fell. Earth opened. Planets tilted. Stars plummeted. And the awful silence.

Chapter 18

Why did you do it?
I don't know.
Have you gone crazy?
Maybe I have.
It was a crazy thing to do.
I know, I know.
*The way that "No" popped out of your mouth—
why?*
I don't know.

It was like the third degree, only he was both
interrogator and suspect, both tough cop and
hounded prisoner, a cruel spotlight pinning him in a
blinding circle of light. All of this in his mind, of
course, as he tossed in his bed, the sheet twisted
around him like a shroud, suffocatingly.

He fought the sheet, filled suddenly with the terror
of claustrophobia, being buried alive. Aware of his
mortality, he turned over again, entangled in the
bedclothes. His pillow fell off the bed, hitting the
floor with a dull thud, like a small body landing there.
He thought of his mother dead in the coffin. When
did death arrive? He had read a magazine article
about heart transplants—even the doctors couldn't
agree on the exact moment that death occurred.
Listen, he told himself, no one can be buried alive
these days, not like in the olden times when there was
no embalming fluid and stuff. Now they removed all
your blood and pumped in chemicals and stuff. To
make certain you were dead. But suppose, let's just
suppose that some small spark in your brain remained

alive, and knew what was going on. His mother. Himself, someday.

He leaped from the bed in terror, flinging the sheet away. His body was moist, oozing perspiration. He sat on the edge of the bed, trembling. Then his feet touched the floor and the cool kiss of the linoleum established reality. The specter of suffocation vanished. He made his way through the darkness to the window, and pulled back the drape. The wind came up, scattering October leaves which fluttered to the ground like doomed and crippled birds.

Why did you do it?

I don't know.

Like a broken record.

Was it because of what Brother Leon does to people, like Bailey, the way he tortures them, tries to make fools of them in front of everybody?

More than that, more than that.

Then what?

He allowed the drape to fall back into place and surveyed the bedroom, squinting into the half-darkness. He padded over to the bed, shivering in the kind of coolness that can only be found in the middle of the night. He listened for night sounds. His father snored in the next room. A car gunned along the street outside. He'd love to be gunning along the street, going someplace, anywhere. *I'm not going to sell the chocolates.* Boy.

He hadn't planned to do any such thing of course. He'd been happy to have the terrible assignment all over with, the assignment completed and life normal once again. Every morning he dreaded the roll call, the necessity of facing Brother Leon, saying *No* and watching Leon's reaction—how the teacher tried to pass off Jerry's rebellion as if it didn't matter, putting on a pathetic pretense of indifference but a pretense that was so transparent, so phony. It had been funny and terrible at the same time, watching Leon call the roll and waiting for his name to be called, and finally his name blazing in the air and the defiant *No*. The teacher might have been able to carry off his act successfully, except for his eyes. His eyes gave him away. His face was always under control but his eyes showed his vulnerability, gave Jerry a glimpse into the hell that was burning inside the teacher. Those moist eyes, the white eyeballs and the diluted blue of his pupils, eyes that reflected everything that went on in the class, reacting to everything. After Jerry had learned that the secret of Brother Leon lurked in his eyes, he became watchful, seeing the way the eyes betrayed the teacher at every turn. And then there came a time when Jerry was tired of it all, tired of watching the teacher, disgusted with the contest of wills that wasn't really a contest because Jerry had no choice. Cruelty sickened Jerry—and the assignment, he realized after a few days, was cruel, even though Archie Costello had insisted that it was only a stunt that everyone would get a kick out of later. And so he had finally waited, impatient for the assignment to come to an end, eager for that silent battle between Brother Leon and himself to be over with. He wanted life to be normal again—football, even his homework, without that daily burden weighing him down. He had felt isolated from the other fellows, separated by the secret he was forced to carry. He'd been tempted once or twice to talk it over with The Goober. In fact, he'd almost done so once when Goob tried to start a conversation. Instead, he'd cautioned himself to hold on for the two weeks, to carry it off, secrecy and all, and be done with it for good. He had met Brother Leon in the corridor late one afternoon after football practice and had seen hate flashing in the teacher's eyes. More than hate: something sick. Jerry had felt soiled, dirty, as if he should run to confession and bare his soul. And he'd consoled himself: when I accept the chocolates and Brother Leon realizes I was only carrying out a Vigil assignment then everything will be fine again.

Then why had he called *No* this morning? He'd wanted to end the ordeal—and then that terrible *No* had issued from his mouth.

In bed once more, Jerry lay without moving, trying to summon sleep. Listening to his father's snores, he thought of how his father was actually sleeping his life away, sleeping even when he was awake, not really alive. And how about me? What was it the guy on the Common had said the other day, his chin resting on the Volkswagen like some grotesque John the Baptist? *You're missing a lot of things in the world.*

He turned over, dismissing his doubts and calling to mind the figure of a girl he'd seen downtown the other day. Her sweater had bulged beautifully, her schoolbooks pressed against her rounded breasts. If my hands were only those books, he'd thought longingly. His hand now curled between his legs, he concentrated on the girl. But for once, it was no good, no good.

Chapter 19

The next morning Jerry found out how a hangover must feel. His eyes burned with fire, fueled by lack of sleep. His head throbbed with shooting pains. His stomach was sensitive to the slightest movement and the lurching of the bus caused strange reactions in his body. It reminded him of when he was a kid and got carsick sometimes on trips to the beach with his parents so that they'd have to stop the car by the side of the road while Jerry either vomited or waited for the storm in his stomach to subside. What added to his troubles this morning was the possibility of a test in geography and he hadn't studied at all last night so wrapped up had he been in the chocolate sale and what had happened in Leon's class. Now, he was paying the penalty for too little sleep and no study— trying to read a lousy geography lesson on a lumbering lurching bus, the morning light dazzling on the white page.

Somebody slipped into the seat beside him.

"Hey, Renault, you got guts, know that?"

Jerry looked up, blinded momentarily as his eyes shifted from the page to the face of the kid who'd spoken to him. He knew him vaguely from school—a junior, maybe. Lighting a cigarette the way all the smokers did despite the "No Smoking" signs, the kid shook his head. "Boy, you really let Leon that bastard have it. Beautiful." He blew out smoke. Jerry's eyes stung.

"Oh," he said, feeling stupid. And surprised. Funny, all this time he had thought of the situation as a private battle between Brother Leon and himself, as if the two of them were alone on the planet. Now, he realized that it had gone beyond that.

"I'm so sick of selling the frigging chocolates," the kid said. He had a terrible case of acne, his face like a relief map. And his fingers were stained with nicotine. "I've been at Trinity two years—I transferred from Monument High when I was a freshman—and Christ I'm getting tired of selling stuff." He tried to blow a smoke ring but failed. Worse than that—the smoke blew back in Jerry's face, stinging his eyes. "If it isn't chocolates, it's Christmas cards. If it isn't Christmas cards, it's soap. If it isn't soap, it's calendars. But you know what?"

"What?" Jerry asked, wanting to get back to his geography.

"I never thought of just saying no. Like you did."

"I've got some studying to do," Jerry said, not knowing what to say, really.

"Boy, you're cool, know that?" the kid said admiringly.

Jerry blushed with pleasure despite himself. Who didn't want to be admired? And yet he felt guilty, knowing that he was accepting the kid's admiration under false pretenses, that he wasn't cool at all, not at all. His head pounded and his stomach moved menacingly and he realized he had to face Brother Leon and the roll call again this morning. And all the mornings to come.

The Goober was waiting for him at the school's entrance, standing tense and troubled among the other fellows waiting for school to start, like prisoners resigned to execution, taking their final drags from cigarettes before the bells began to ring. The Goober motioned Jerry aside. Jerry followed him guiltily. He realized that Goober wasn't the cheerful happy-go-lucky kid he'd known when school first started. What had happened? He'd been so wrapped up in his own concerns that he hadn't bothered about Goob.

"Jeez, Jerry, what did you do it for?" Goober asked, drawing him away from the others.

"Do what?"

But he knew what Goober meant.

"The chocolates."

"I don't know, Goob," Jerry said. It was no use faking out Goober the way he had faked out that kid on the bus. "That's the truth—I don't know."

"You're asking for trouble, Jerry. Brother Leon spells trouble."

"Look, Goob," Jerry said, wanting to reassure his friend, wanting to wipe that look of concern from his face. "It's not the end of the world. Four hundred kids in this school are going to sell chocolates. What does it matter if I don't?"

"It's not that simple, Jerry. Brother Leon won't let you get away with it."

The warning bell sounded. Cigarettes were flipped into the gutter or mashed into the sand-filled receptacle near the door. Last drags were inhaled lingeringly. Guys who'd been sitting in cars listening to rock on the radio switched them off and slammed the doors behind them.

"Nice going, kid," somebody said, hurrying by, the pat on the ass Trinity's traditional gesture of friendship. Jerry didn't see who it was.

"Keep it up, Jerry." This, a corner-of-the-mouth whisper from Adamo who hated Leon with a vengeance.

"See how the word is spreading?" Goober hissed. "What's more important—football and your marks or the lousy chocolate sale?"

The bell rang again. It meant two minutes left to get to your locker and then to your homeroom.

A senior by the name of Benson approached them. Seniors were trouble for freshmen. It was better to be ignored by them than to be noticed. But Benson was clearly headed in their direction. He was a nut, known for his lack of inhibitions, his complete disregard of the rules.

As he neared Jerry and Goober, he began a Jimmy Cagney imitation, shooting his cuffs and hunching his shoulders. "Hey, there, guy. I wouldn't . . . I wouldn't be in your shoes . . . I wouldn't be in your shoes for a thou, boy, a mill . . ." He punched Jerry playfully on the arm.

"You couldn't fit those shoes anyway, Benson," somebody yelled. And Benson danced away, Sammy Davis now, wide grin, feet tapping, body whirling.

Walking up the stairs, Goober said, "Do me a favor, Jerry. Take the chocolates today."

"I can't, Goob."

"Why not?"

"I just can't. I'm committed now."

"The goddam Vigils," Goober said.

Jerry had never heard Goober swear before. He'd always been a mild kind of kid, rolling with the punches, loose and carefree, running around the track while the other kids sat uptight during practice sessions.

"It's not The Vigils, Goob. They're not in it anymore. It's me."

They stopped at Jerry's locker.

"All right," Goober said, resigned, knowing it was useless to pursue the subject any further at the moment. Jerry felt sad suddenly because Goober looked so troubled, like an old man heaped with all the sorrows of the world, his thin face drawn and haggard, his eyes haunted, as if he had awakened from a nightmare he couldn't forget.

Jerry opened his locker. He had thumbtacked a poster to the back wall of the locker on the first day of school. The poster showed a wide expanse of beach, a sweep of sky with a lone star glittering far away. A man walked on the beach, a small solitary figure in all that immensity. At the bottom of the poster, these words appeared—*Do I dare disturb the universe?* By Eliot, who wrote the Waste Land thing they were studying in English. Jerry wasn't sure of the poster's meaning. But it had moved him mysteriously. It was traditional at Trinity for everyone to decorate the interior of his locker with a poster. Jerry chose this one.

He had no time now to ponder the poster any longer. The final bell rang and he had thirty seconds to get to class.

"Adamo?"

"Two."

"Beauvais?"

"Three."

It was a different roll call this morning, a new melody, a new tempo, as if Brother Leon were the conductor and the class the members of a verbal orchestra, but something wrong with the beat, something wrong with the entire proceedings, as if the members of the orchestra were controlling the pace and not the conductor. No sooner would Brother Leon call out a name than the response came immediately, before Leon had time to make a notation in the ledger. It was the kind of spontaneous game that developed in classes without premeditation, everyone falling into a sudden conspiracy. The quickness of the responses kept Brother Leon busy at his desk, head bent, pencil furiously scribbling. Jerry was glad that he wouldn't have to look into those watery eyes.

"LeBlanc?"

"One."

"Malloran?"

"Two."

Names and numbers sizzled in the air and Jerry began to notice something curious about it. All the ones and twos, and an occasional three. But no fives, no tens. And Brother Leon's head still bent, concentrating on the ledger. And finally—

"Renault."

It would be so easy, really, to yell "Yes." To say, "Give me the chocolates to sell, Brother Leon." So easy to be like the others, not to have to confront those terrible eyes every morning. Brother Leon finally looked up. The tempo of the roll call had broken.

"No," Jerry said.

He was swept with sadness, a sadness deep and penetrating, leaving him desolate like someone washed up on a beach, a lone survivor in a world full of strangers.

Chapter 20

"At this period of history, man began to learn more about his environment—"

Suddenly, pandemonium reigned. The class exploded in frantic motion. Brother Jacques looked aghast. The boys leaped from their chairs, performed an insane jig, jumping up and down as if to the beat of unheard music, all of this in complete silence— although the sound of their jogging feet was noisy enough—and then sat down again, frozen-faced, as if nothing had happened.

Obie watched the teacher sourly. Brother Jacques was obviously bewildered. Bewildered? Hell, he was on the edge of panic. The ritual had been going on for a week now and it would continue until the cue was heard no more. In the meantime, the class would suddenly erupt into a confusion of waving arms and jogging legs, unsettling poor Brother. Of course, Brother Jacques was easy to unsettle—he was new and young and sensitive, raw meat for Archie. And he evidently didn't know what to do about it and so he didn't do anything, figuring apparently that the thing would run its course and why risk a futile showdown when it was obviously a prank. What else could it be? Funny, Obie thought, how everybody—the kids as well as the teachers—knew these stunts were planned or carried out by The Vigils and yet they still maintained that air of mystery, refusing to acknowledge it all. He wondered why. Obie had been involved in so many Vigil assignments that he'd lost count of them and he was continually amazed at how they got away with it all the time. In fact, he'd been getting tired of the assignments, of playing nursemaid for Archie and his trigger man as well. He was tired of being the fixer, making certain the assignment went off on schedule in order to maintain Archie's big shot reputation. Like the Room Nineteen assignment when he'd had to creep in there and help the kid Goober take the place apart—all that work so that Archie and The Vigils would look good. Even this particular assignment involved him—if Brother Jacques failed to come up with the cue, then Obie had to find a way to feed it to him.

The cue was the word "environment." As Archie had said when he announced the assignment, "The world today is concerned with ecology, the environment, our natural resources. We at Trinity also ought to get involved in this environment thing. You guys," he said, indicating the fourteen students of Grade Twelve Class II, of whom Obie was a member, "will carry on our environmental campaign. Let's say Brother Jacques' U.S. History class—history should be concerned with environment, shouldn't it? Now, whenever Brother Jacques says the word 'environment,' here's what happens . . ." And Archie had outlined the instructions.

"Suppose he doesn't use the word?" someone asked.

Archie looked toward Obie. "Oh, Brother Jacques will use the word. I'm sure somebody—Obie, maybe—will ask a question that will produce the word. Won't you, Obie?"

Obie had nodded, disguising his disgust. What the hell was Archie involving him in an assignment at this stage of the game for? He was a senior, for crying out loud. He was secretary of the goddam Vigils, for crying out loud. Jesus, how he hated Archie, that bastard.

A new kid, a transfer from Monument High, asked, "What happens when Brother Jacques finds out we're putting him on? When he finds out that the key word is environment?"

"Then he stops using it," Archie said. "Which is the point of the whole damn thing. I'm getting sick and tired of all this environment crap—and at least we'll have one teacher in the frigging school who'll cross it off his vocabulary list."

For his part, Obie was getting sick and tired of Archie, of picking up the pieces behind him, of performing those little services—like Room Nineteen or cueing in Brother Jacques, feeding him a question that could only lead to the word "environment" in the answer. Anyway he was getting fed up with the entire deal. And he was also biding his time, waiting for Archie to overreach himself, to make a mistake. The black box was always there and who could tell when Archie's luck would run out?

"In any discussion of the environment . . ."

Here we go again, Obie thought in disgust as he found himself leaping up and down like a madman, jogging his heart out, hating every minute of the damn thing. And his energy was wearing down.

Brother Jacques used the word "environment" five more times in the next fifteen minutes. Obie and the other guys were practically wiped out from all that jumping up and down, weary, out of breath, their legs beginning to ache.

When Brother Jacques used the word a sixth time and a weary battalion of students struggled to their feet to perform their task, Obie saw a small smile play on the lips of the teacher. And he knew immediately what had happened. Archie, that bastard, must have tipped Brother Jacques off, anonymously, of course, to what was going on. And the teacher had turned the tables. It was now the teacher who was in command, making the guys jump up and down until they almost collapsed in exhaustion.

When they left the classroom, there was Archie leaning against the wall, that smirk of triumph on his face. The other guys didn't realize what had happened. But Obie did. He gave Archie a look that would shrivel anybody else, but Archie just kept that silly smile on his face.

Obie stalked off, insulted, injured. You bastard, he thought, I owe you for that.

Chapter 21

Kevin Chartier had gone to seven houses after school and hadn't sold a box. Mrs. Connors next to the dry cleaners had told him to come back at the end of the month when her Social Security check came from the government but he didn't have the heart to tell her that it would probably be too late by then. A dog chased him halfway home. It was like one of those terrible dogs the Nazis used for hunting down concentration camp prisoners who escaped in those old TV pictures. At home, disgusted, he telephoned his best friend, Danny Arcangelo.

"How'd you make out, Danny?" Kevin asked, trying to ignore his mother who stood near the phone making sounds at him. Kevin had learned long ago to translate whatever she was saying into gibberish. She could talk her head off now and the words reached his ears without meaning. A wild trick.

"I made out terrible," Danny whined. He always sounded like he had to blow his nose. "I sold one box—to my aunt."

"The one with diabetes?"

Danny howled. One thing about Danny, he was a great audience. But not Kevin's mother. She was still chattering away. Kevin knew what was bugging her. She never wanted him to eat when he was on the telephone. His mother didn't realize that eating wasn't something you did *separately*. Eating went along with whatever you happened to be doing at the time. You could eat doing anything. Well, almost anything. It's not polite to be on the phone with your mouth full of food, she always said. But right this minute, Danny also had *his* mouth full of food at the other end of the line. So who the hell was being impolite to who? Or whom? Screw it.

"I think maybe that Renault kid's got the right idea, after all," Kevin said, his mouth thick with peanut butter which, he wished he could explain to his mother, gave his words more resonance, like a disc jockey's.

"The freshman who's giving Brother Leon a hard time?"

"Yeah. He came flat out and said he wasn't going to sell the junk."

"I thought it was a Vigils thing," Danny said tentatively.

"It *was*," Kevin said, leering in triumph as his mother gave up and went into the kitchen. "But now it's something else." He wondered whether he was saying too much. "He was supposed to take the chocolates a couple of days ago. The assignment was over. But he still refused to take them."

Kevin could hear Danny chewing like a madman.

"What're you eating, anyway? Sounds delicious."

Danny howled again. "Chocolates. I bought a box myself. The least I could do for good old Trinity."

An awkward silence fell between them. Kevin was in line to become a member of The Vigils next year when he became a junior. No one could be sure, of course, but there had been some hints from the guys. His best friend, Danny, knew about the possibility—and he also knew that there was a certain secrecy about The Vigils that had to be maintained. They usually avoided Vigil talk although Kevin often had inside information about assignments and stuff and he often fed it to Danny in bits and pieces, finding it hard not to show off a bit. Yet he was always afraid that

Danny might say something about The Vigils to some other guys, strictly by accident, and screw up the whole situation. They had reached that point now in their conversation.

"What happens now?" Danny asked, still unsure about poking his nose in but made reckless by curiosity.

"I don't know," Kevin said truthfully. "Maybe The Vigils will take some action. Maybe they don't give a hell. But I'll tell you one thing."

"What?"

"I'm getting sick of selling stuff. Jeez, my father's starting to call me 'my son, the salesman.'"

Danny guffawed again. Kevin was a natural mimic. "Yeah, I know what you mean. I'm getting tired of this selling crap. The kid's probably got the right idea."

Kevin agreed.

"For two cents, I'd stop," Danny said.

"Got change for a nickel?" Kevin said, all in fun, of course, but thinking how beautiful—bee-yoo-tee-full—it would be not to have to sell anything anymore. He looked up to find his mother approaching him again, her mouth moving and sounds coming out, and he sighed, tuning her out, like shutting off the sound on television while the picture remained.

"Know what?" Howie Anderson asked.

"What?" Richy Rondell answered, lazily, dreamily. He was watching a girl approach. Fantastic looking. Tight sweater, clinging, low-slung jeans. Jesus.

"I think the Renault kid is right about the chocolates," Howie said. He'd seen the girl too, as she moved along the sidewalk in front of Crane's Drug Store. But it didn't break his train of thought. Watching girls and devouring them with your eyes—

rape by eyeball—was something you did automatically. "I'm not going to sell them anymore, either."

The girl paused to look at newspapers in a metal rack outside the store. Richy gazed at her with wistful lust. Suddenly he realized what Howie had said. "You're not?" he asked. Without taking his eyes off the girl—her back was turned now and he feasted himself on her rounded jeans—he pondered the meaning of what Howie had said, sensing the importance of the moment. Howie Anderson wasn't just another Trinity student. He was president of the junior class, an unusual guy. High honor student and varsity guard on the football team. He could also hold his own in the ring and almost knocked out that monster Carter in the intramural matches last year. His hand could shoot up in class to show he had the answer to a tough question. But that same hand could also shoot out and floor you if you screwed around with him. An intellectual roughneck—that's what one teacher had called him a while back. A freshman-nobody like Renault not selling chocolates—that was nothing. But Howie Anderson—that was *something*.

"It's the principle of the thing," Howie went on.

Richy plunged his hand in his pocket, grabbing shamelessly, something he couldn't resist whenever he got excited, about a girl or anything else.

"What principle, Howie?"

"This is what I mean," Howie said. "We pay tuition to go to Trinity, don't we? Right. Hell, I'm not even a Catholic, a lot of guys aren't, but they sell us a bill of goods that Trinity is the best prep school for college you can find around here. There's a case full of trophies in the auditorium—debating, football, boxing. And what happens? They turn us into salesmen. I have to listen to all this religious crap and even go to chapel. And sell chocolates on top of it all." He spat and a beautiful spray hit a mailbox, dripping down like a teardrop. "And now along comes a freshman. A *child*. He says no. He says 'I'm not going to sell the chocolates.' Simple. Beautiful. Something I never thought of before—just stop selling them."

Richy watched the girl drifting away.

"I'm with you, Howie. As of this moment, no more selling of chocolates." The girl was almost out of sight now, blocked from view by other people walking by. "Want to make it official? I mean, call a meeting of the class?"

Howie pondered the question.

"No, Richy. This is the age of do your thing. Let everybody do his thing. If a kid wants to sell, let him. If he doesn't, the same thing applies."

Howie's voice rang with authority, as if he was delivering a pronouncement to the world. Richy listened with a kind of awe. He was glad that Howie let him hang around—maybe some of Howie's leadership qualities would rub off on him. His eyes went to the street again, looking for another girl to enjoy.

The odor of sweat filled the air—a gym's sour perfume. Even though the place was deserted, the aftermath of that final period of calisthenics lingered, the stink of boy sweat; armpits and feet. And the rotten smell of old sneakers. That was one of the reasons why Archie had never been attracted to sports—he hated the secretions of the human body, pee or perspiration. He hated athletics because it speeded up the process of sweat. He couldn't stand the sight of greasy, oozing athletes drenched in their own body fluids. At least football players wore uniforms, but boxers wore only the trunks. Take a guy like Carter, bulging with muscles, every pore oozing sweat. Put him in boxing trunks and the sight was almost obscene. That's why Archie avoided the gym. He was a legend in the school for dreaming up ways of avoiding Phys. Ed. But he was here now waiting for Obie. Obie had left a note in Archie's locker. *Meet me in the gym after last period.* Obie loved dramatics. He also knew that Archie despised the gym and yet asked to be met here. Oh, Obie, how you must hate me, Archie thought, undisturbed by the knowledge. It was good to have people hate you—it kept you sharp. And then when you put the needle in them, the way he did constantly to Obie, you felt justified, you didn't have to worry about your conscience.

But at this minute he was getting annoyed with Obie. Where the hell was he? Sitting down on one of the bleacher seats, Archie found a sudden and unexpected peace in the deserted gymnasium. His moments of peace were becoming less frequent all the time. The Vigils—those assignments, the constant pressure. More assignments due and everybody waiting for what Archie would come up with. And Archie hollow and empty sometimes, no ideas at all. And his lousy marks. He was certain to flunk English this term, simply because English was mostly reading and he didn't have time anymore to spend four or five hours every night reading a lousy book. Anyway, between The Vigils and worrying about his marks, he didn't seem to have any time to himself anymore, not even time for girls, no time to hang around Miss Jerome's, the girls' high school across town where, when school let out for the day, you could let your eyes devour some luscious sights and usually talk one of them into the car, for a ride home. With detours. Instead, here he was every day, involved with assignments and homework, juggling all this activity and then getting stupid notes from Obie. Meet me in the gym . . .

Finally, Obie made his entrance. He didn't just walk in. He had to make a production out of it. He had to peek around the door and sniff the air and act like he was the spy coming in from the cold, for Christ's sake.

"Hey, Obie, I'm over here," Archie called dryly.

"Hi, Archie," Obie said as his leather heels clicked on the gym floor. There was a rule in the school—only sneakers on the gym floor but everybody ignored it except when there was a brother around.

"What do you want, Obie?" Archie asked, getting down to business without preliminaries, keeping his voice flat and dry as the Sahara. The fact that he had showed up for the meeting had been an admission of curiosity. Archie didn't want to overdo it by acting too eager for Obie's company and whatever he had to say. "I haven't much time. Important things await."

"This is important too," Obie said. Obie had a thin sharp face with a permanent worried look. That's why he was such an obvious stooge, an errand boy. The kind of kid you couldn't help kicking when he was down. And you also knew this—that he would get up again and vow revenge and never have the nerve or the know-how to take that revenge. "Remember that kid Renault? The chocolate assignment?"

"What about him?"

"He's still not selling the chocolates."

"So?"

"So—remember? His orders were not to sell them for ten school days. Okay. So the ten days came and went and he's still saying no."

"So what?"

This is what infuriated Obie—the way Archie tried so hard not to be impressed, to always play it cool.

You could tell him that The Bomb was going to be dropped and he'd probably say "So what?" It got under Obie's skin, mostly because he suspected that it was an act, that Archie wasn't as cool as he pretended to be. And Obie was awaiting his chance to find out.

"Well, there's all kinds of rumors around the school. First of all, a lot of kids think that The Vigils are in on the deal, that Renault still isn't selling them because he's still carrying out the assignment. Then there are some kids who know the assignment is over and think that Renault is leading some kind of revolt against the sale. They say Brother Leon is climbing the wall every day . . ."

"Beautiful," Archie said, showing reaction to Obie's news at last.

"Every morning Leon calls the roll and every day this kid, a freshman, sits there, and won't sell the goddam chocolates."

"Beautiful."

"You said that."

"Continue," Archie said, ignoring Obie's sarcasm.

"Well, I understand that the sale is going lousy. Nobody wants to sell the chocolates in the first place and it's turned into a kind of farce in some classes."

Obie sat down on the bleacher seat beside Archie, pausing to let the report sink in.

Archie sniffed the air and said, "This gymnasium stinks." Pretending indifference to Obie's report but his thoughts racing, pondering the possibilities.

Obie poured it on. "The eager beavers, the brown nosers are out selling chocolates like madmen. So are Leon's pets, his special boys. So are the kids who still believe in school spirit." He sighed. "Anyway, there's a lot going on."

Archie was busy contemplating the far side of the gym, as if something interesting was going on over there. Obie followed his gaze—nothing. "Well, what do you think, Archie?" he asked.

"What do you mean—what do I think?"

"The situation. Renault. Brother Leon. The chocolates. The kids out there taking sides . . ."

"We'll see, we'll see," Archie said. "I don't know whether The Vigils should get involved or not." He yawned.

That phony yawn irritated Obie. "Hey, look, Archie. The Vigils are involved whether you know it or not."

"What are you talking about?"

"Look, you told the kid to refuse the chocolates in the first place. That's what started all this stuff. But the kid went beyond that. He was supposed to start selling after the assignment was over. So, now he's defying The Vigils. And a lot of guys know that. We are involved, Archie, whether we want to be or not."

Obie could see that he had scored. He saw something flash in Archie's eyes, like looking at a blank window and observing a ghost peeking out.

"Nobody defies The Vigils, Obie . . ."

"That's what Renault's doing."

". . . and gets away with it."

Archie had that dreamy look again and his lower lip drooped. "Here's what to do. Arrange to have Renault appear before The Vigils. Check up on the sale—get the totals, facts and figures."

"Right," Obie said, writing in his notebook. As much as he hated Archie, he loved to see him when he was swinging into action. Obie decided to add more fuel to the flames. "Another thing, Archie. Didn't The Vigils promise Leon way back they'd back him in the chocolate sale?"

Obie had scored again. Archie turned to him, surprise scrawled on his face. But he recovered quickly. "Let me worry about Leon. You just run your errands, Obie."

God, how Obie hated the son of a bitch. He snapped his notebook shut and left Archie sitting there in the polluted atmosphere of the gymnasium.

Chapter 22

Brian Cochran couldn't believe his eyes. He went through the totals again, double-checking, making sure he hadn't screwed up. Frowning, biting the pencil, he pondered the results of his arithmetic—sales were dropping at an alarming rate. For a week now, they'd been going steadily downward. But yesterday, the sharpest drop of all.

What would Brother Leon say? That was Brian's main concern. Brian hated the job of treasurer because it was such a drag but mostly because it brought him into personal contact with Brother Leon. Leon gave Brian the chills. The teacher was unpredictable, moody. He was never satisfied. Complaints, complaints—your sevens look like nines, Cochran. Or, you spelled Sulkey's name wrong—it's Sulkey with an *e*, Cochran.

Brian had been lucky recently. Brother Leon had stopped checking the totals on a daily basis, almost as if he anticipated the bad news the figures contained and wanted to avoid finding out about it definitely. Today was zero hour, however. He had told Brian to prepare the totals. Now Brian waited for the teacher to show up. He'd go ape when he saw the figures. Brian shivered, actually shivered! He'd read how in historic times they killed the bearer of bad news. He had the feeling that Brother Leon was that kind of character, that he would need a scapegoat and Brian would be closest at hand. Brian sighed, tired of it all, wishing he were outside on this beautiful October day, gunning around in the old Chevy his father had bought him when school started. He loved the car. "Me and my Chevy," Brian hummed to the tune of a song he'd heard on the radio.

"Well, Brian."

Brother Leon had a way of sneaking up on you. Brian leaped and almost came to attention. That's the kind of lousy effect the teacher had on him.

"Yes, Brother Leon."

"Sit, sit," Leon said, and took his place behind the desk. Leon was sweating, as usual. He had removed his black jacket and his shirt was stained with wetness at the armpits. A faint smell of perspiration reached Brian.

"The totals are bad," Brian said, plunging, wanting to get it over with, wanting to get out of the school, this office, Leon's suffocating presence. And feeling simultaneously a twist of triumph—Leon was such a rat, let him have some bad news for a change.

"Bad?"

"The sales are down. Below last year's. And last year, the quota was half of what has to be sold this year."

"I know, I know," Leon said sharply, swiveling away in his desk chair as if Brian weren't important enough to be addressed directly. "Are you sure of your figures? You're not exactly a whiz at adding and subtracting, Cochran."

Brian flushed with anger. He was tempted to throw the master sheet at the Brother but held back. Nobody defied Brother Leon. Not Brian Cochran, anyway, who only wanted to get out of here.

"I double-checked everything," Brian said, keeping his voice even.

Silence.

The floor vibrated under Brian's feet. The boxing

club working out in the gym, maybe, doing calisthenics or the other stuff boxers did.

"Cochran. Read off the names of the boys who have reached or surpassed their quota."

Brian reached for the lists. A simple task because Brother Leon insisted that all kinds of cross-indexed lists be kept so that you could tell at a glance just where students stood.

"Sulkey, sixty-two. Maronia, fifty-eight. LeBlanc, fifty-two—"

"Slower, slower," Brother Leon said, still facing away from Brian. "Begin again and slower."

It was spooky but Brian began again, pronouncing the names more exactly, pausing between names and figures.

"Sulkey . . . sixty-two . . . Maronia . . . fifty-eight . . . LeBlanc . . . fifty-two . . . Caroni . . . fifty . . ."

Brother Leon was nodding his head, as if listening to a beautiful symphony, as if lovely sounds filled the air.

"Fontaine . . . fifty . . ." Brian paused. "Those are the only ones who either made the quota or topped it, Brother Leon."

"Read the others. There are many students who sold over forty. Read those names . . ." His face still turned away, his body slouched in the chair.

Brian shrugged and continued, calling out the names in singsong fashion, with measured pauses, letting his voice linger over the names and numbers, a weird litany here in the quiet office. When he ran out of the sales in the forties, he continued into the thirties and Brother Leon did not tell him to halt.

". . . Sullivan . . . thirty-three . . . Charlton . . . thirty-two . . . Kelly . . . thirty-two . . . Ambrose . . . thirty-one . . ."

Once in a while Brian looked up to see Brother Leon's head nodding, as if he were communicating with someone unseen or only himself. While the recitation went on—from the thirties into the twenties.

His eyes running ahead, Brian saw that he was in for trouble. After he was through with the twenties and the teens, there was a big leap. He wondered how Brother Leon would react to the small returns. Brian began to grow warm and his voice turned hoarse. He needed a drink of water, not only to relieve the dryness of his throat but to ease the tension of his neck muscles.

"... Antonelli ... fifteen ... Lombard ... thirteen . . ." He cleared his throat, breaking the rhythm, interrupting the flow of the report. A deep breath and then, "Cartier . . . six." He shot a look at Brother Leon but the teacher hadn't moved. His hands were clasped together, resting in his lap. "Cartier . . . he only sold six because he's been out of school. Appendicitis. He's been in the hospital . . ."

Brother Leon waved his hand, a gesture that said, "I understand, it doesn't matter." At least, that's what Brian figured it meant. And the gesture also seemed to mean "continue." He looked at the last name on the list.

"Renault . . . zero."

The pause. No names left.

"Renault . . . zero," Brother Leon said, his voice a sibilant whisper. "Can you imagine that, Cochran? A Trinity boy who has refused to sell the chocolates? Do you know what's happened, Cochran? Do you know why the sales have fallen off?"

"I don't know, Brother Leon," Brian said lamely.

"The boys have become infected, Cochran. Infected

by a disease we could call apathy. A terrible disease. Difficult to cure."

What was he talking about?

"Before a cure can be found, the cause must be discovered. But in this case, Cochran, the cause is known. The carrier of the disease is known."

Brian knew what he was getting at now. Leon figured that Renault was the cause, the carrier of the disease. As if reading Brian's mind, Leon whispered "Renault . . . Renault . . ."

Like a mad scientist plotting revenge in an underground laboratory, for crying out loud.

Chapter 23

"I'm quitting the team, Jerry."

"Why, Goob? I thought you liked football. We're just starting to click. You made a sensational catch yesterday."

They were headed for the bus stop. Today was Wednesday—no practice on Wednesday. Jerry was looking forward to arriving at the bus stop. There was a girl, beautiful, with hair like maple syrup. He'd seen her there a few times and she'd smiled at him. One day he'd gotten close enough to read her name on one of the schoolbooks she held in her arms. Ellen Barrett. Someday he'd get up the courage to speak to her. *Hi, Ellen.* Or call her on the telephone. Today maybe.

"Let's run," Goober said.

Off they went on a mad and awkward sprint. Their books prevented them from running with grace and abandon. But the mere act of running cheered up The Goober.

"Are you serious about quitting the team?" Jerry asked, his voice higher than usual, strained from the running.

"I've got to quit, Jerry." He was glad that his own voice was normal, unaffected by the running.

They turned into Gate Street.

"Why?" Jerry asked, launching himself into Gate Street with a burst of speed.

Their feet pounded on the pavement.

How can I tell him, Goob wondered.

Jerry had shot ahead. He glanced back over his

shoulder, his face crimson with effort. "Why, damn it?"

The Goober caught up to him with a slight acceleration of his pace. He could easily have slid past him.

"Did you hear what happened to Brother Eugene?" The Goober asked.

"He got transferred," Jerry answered, squeezing the words out of himself like toothpaste from a tube. He was in good shape because of football but he wasn't a runner and didn't know the tricks.

"I heard he's gone on sick leave," Goober said.

"What's the difference?" Jerry replied. He took a deep sweet breath. "Hey, my legs are okay but my arms are killing me." He carried two books in each hand.

"Keep running."

"You're some kind of nut," Jerry said, humoring him.

They were approaching the intersection of Green and Gate. Seeing Jerry's discomfort, The Goober slackened his pace. "They say Brother Eugene's never been the same since Room Nineteen. They say he's all broken up over it. Can't eat or sleep. The shock."

"Rumors," Jerry gasped. "Hey, Goob, my lungs are burning up. I'm in a state of collapse."

"I know how he feels, Jerry. I know how a thing like that can drive somebody up a wall." Shouting the words into the wind. They had never discussed the destruction of Room Nineteen although Jerry knew about Goober's involvement. "Some people can't stand cruelty, Jerry. And that was a cruel thing to do to a guy like Eugene . . ."

"What's Brother Eugene got to do with not playing football?" Jerry asked, really gasping now, really sweating, his lungs threatening to burst and his arms aching from the burden of the books.

Goober put on the brakes, slackening his pace, coming finally to a halt. Jerry blew air out of his mouth as he collapsed on the edge of someone's front lawn. His chest rose and fell like human bellows.

The Goober sat on the curbstone, his legs jack-knifed, his feet in the gutter. He studied the leaves clustered beneath his feet. He was trying to find a way to explain to Jerry the connection between Brother Eugene and Room Nineteen and not playing football anymore. He knew there was a connection but it was hard to put into words.

"Look, Jerry. There's something rotten in that school. More than rotten." He groped for the word and found it but didn't want to use it. The word didn't fit the surroundings, the sun and the bright October afternoon. It was a midnight word, a howling wind word.

"The Vigils?" Jerry asked. He'd lain back on the lawn and was looking at the blue sky, the hurrying autumn clouds.

"That's part of it," The Goober said. He wished they were still running. "Evil," he said.

"What did you say?"

Crazy. Jerry would think he'd flipped. "Nothing," Goober said. "Anyway, I'm not going to play football. It's a personal thing, Jerry." He took a deep breath. "And I'm not going out for track next spring."

They sat in silence.

"What's the matter, Goob?" Jerry finally asked, voice troubled and loaded with concern.

"It's what they do to us, Jerry." It was easier saying the words because they weren't looking at each other, both staring ahead. "What they did to me that night in the classroom—I was crying like a baby, something

I never thought I'd do again in my life. And what they did to Brother Eugene, wrecking his room, wrecking *him* . . ."

"Aw, take it easy, Goob."

"And what they're doing to you—the chocolates."

"It's all a game, Goob. Think of it as fun and games. Let them have their fun. Brother Eugene must have been on the borderline, anyway . . ."

"It's more than fun and games, Jerry. Anything that can make you cry and send a teacher away—tip him over the borderline—that's more than just fun and games."

They sat there for a long time, Jerry on the lawn and Goober on the curb. Jerry knew he'd be too late now to see the girl—Ellen Barrett—but he felt that Goober needed his presence at this moment. Some of the guys from school passed by and called to them. A bus came along and halted. The driver was disgusted when The Goober shook his head that they didn't want a ride.

After a while, Goober said, "Sell the chocolates, Jerry, will you?"

Jerry said, "Play football."

Goober shook his head. "I'm not giving anything more to Trinity. Not football, not running, not anything."

They sat in sadness. Finally, they gathered their books, got up, and walked in silence to the bus stop.

The girl wasn't there.

Chapter 24

"You're in trouble," Brother Leon said.

You're in trouble, not me, Archie wanted to answer. But didn't. He had never spoken to Leon on the telephone before and the disembodied voice at the other end of the line had caught him off balance.

"What's the matter?" Archie asked cautiously, but knowing, of course.

"The chocolates," Leon said. "They're not selling. The entire sale is in jeopardy." Leon's breath filled in the gaps between the words as if he'd been running a long distance. Was he on the edge of panic?

"How bad is it?" Archie asked, relaxing now, stalling. He knew how bad it was.

"It could hardly be worse. The sale is more than half finished. The initial push is over. There is no momentum. Half the chocolates haven't been sold yet. And the sales are virtually at a standstill." Leon paused in the recital. "You're not being very effective, Archie."

Archie shook his head in grudging admiration. Here was Leon with his back to the wall and still he was on the offensive. *You're not being very effective, Archie.*

"You mean the finances are bad?" Archie taunted, launching his own offensive. To Leon, it may have sounded like a shot in the dark but it wasn't. The question was based on information Archie had received that afternoon from Brian Cochran.

Cochran had stopped him in the second-floor corridor and motioned Archie into an empty classroom. Archie had been reluctant. The kid was Leon's bookkeeper and probably his stooge. But the information revealed that Cochran was no stooge for Leon.

"Listen, I think Leon's in deep trouble. There's more than chocolates involved here, Archie."

Archie resented Cochran's familiarity, the use of his name. But he didn't say anything, curious about what the kid had to say.

"I overheard Leon talking with Brother Jacques. Jacques was trying to back him into a corner. He kept mentioning something about Leon abusing his power of attorney. That he'd overextended the school's finances. That was his exact word, 'overextended.' The chocolates came into it. Something about twenty thousand boxes and Leon paying cash in advance. I didn't hear all of it . . . I got out of there before they could find out I was around . . ."

"So what do you think, Cochran?" Archie asked, although he knew. Leon needed at least twenty thousand dollars to draw even with the school.

"I think Leon bought the chocolates with money that he wasn't supposed to use. Now, the sale's going lousy and he's caught in the middle. And Brother Jacques smells a rat . . ."

"Jacques is sharp," Archie said, remembering how Jacques had acted on Archie's anonymous tip about the word "environment"—making the class look ridiculous, Obie among them. "Good job, Cochran."

Cochran beamed at the praise. Encouraged, he drew some sheets of paper out of a book he was carrying. "Take a look at this stuff sometime, Archie. It's facts and figures about this year's sale and last year's. And it's all bad. I think Leon's on the run . . ."

But Cochran really didn't know Leon, Archie realized now as the teacher's voice came vibrantly over the line. Leon had ignored Archie's taunt about finances and had resumed his offensive.

"I thought you had influence, Archie. You and your . . . friends."

"It's not my sale, Brother Leon."

"It's your sale in more ways than you realize, Archie," Leon said, sighing. It was his phony sigh, his usual act. "You played games at the beginning, Archie, with that freshman Renault and got yourself involved. Now, the game has backfired."

Renault. Archie thought of the kid's refusal to sell, his ridiculous defiance. He remembered the triumph in Obie's voice when he'd told him of Renault's action—it's your move, Archie baby. But it was always Archie's move anyway.

And he moved now. "Just a minute," he told Brother Leon. He put down the phone and went to the den where he removed Cochran's data from his U.S. History textbook. Returning to the phone, he said, "I've got some figures here about last year's sale. Do you know they barely sold all the chocolates last year? Kids are getting tired of selling stuff. Last year, it took a lot of prizes and bonuses to get the kids to sell only twenty-five boxes at one dollar a box. And this year they're stuck with fifty boxes at two dollars each. That's why the sale is falling apart—not because of games being played."

Brother Leon's breathing filled the line, as if he were some kind of obscene phone caller.

"Archie," he said, whispering, menace in the whisper, as if the information he had to impart was too terrible to be spoken aloud. "I don't care about fun and games. I don't care whether it's Renault or your precious organization or the state of the economy. All I know is that the chocolates aren't being sold. And I want them sold!"

"Any ideas about how?" Archie said, fighting for time again. Funny, he knew Leon was in a precarious position and yet there was always the danger of underestimating him. He still had the authority of the school behind him. Archie had only his wits and a bunch of guys who were all big zeroes without him.

"Perhaps you should begin with Renault," Leon said. "I think he should be made to say 'yes' instead of 'no.' I'm convinced, Archie, that he's become a symbol to those who would like to see the sale defeated. The malingerers, the malcontents—they always rally around a rebel. Renault must sell the chocolates. And you, The Vigils—yes, I'm saying the name aloud—The Vigils must throw their full weight behind the sale . . ."

"That's quite an order, Brother."

"You've spoken the correct word, Archie. *Order*—it is an order."

"I don't know what you mean, Brother."

"I'll make it clear, Archie. If the sale goes down the drain, you and The Vigils also go down the drain. Believe me . . ."

Archie was about to respond, tempted to let Leon know that he had learned about the financial trouble, but he didn't get the chance. Leon, that bastard, had already hung up and the dial tone exploded in Archie's ear.

Chapter 25

The summons looked like a ransom note—letters cut out of a newspaper or magazine. *vIgiL MeEtinG tWO-THirTy*. The wackiness of the note, those crazy letters, made it seem childish and ridiculous. But that same touch of the childish also gave it an air of something not quite rational, faintly threatening and mocking. That was the special quality of The Vigils, of course, and Archie Costello.

Thirty minutes later, Jerry stood before The Vigils in the storage room. The nearby gym was occupied by fellows either practicing basketball or boxing calisthenics and the walls echoed with thuddings, bouncings and whistles blowing, like a grotesque sound track. Nine or ten Vigil members were present, including Carter who was getting tired of this Vigil crap, especially when it meant he had to miss boxing, and Obie who looked forward to the meeting with pleasure, wondering how Archie would proceed. Archie sat behind the card table. The table was covered with a scarf of purple and gold—the school colors. In the exact center of the table: a box of chocolates.

"Renault," Archie said softly.

Instinctively, Jerry came to attention, squaring his shoulders, sucking in his stomach, and immediately disgusted with himself.

"Have a chocolate, Renault?"

Jerry shook his head, sighing. He thought wistfully of the guys out on the football field in the sweet fresh wind, tossing the ball around before practice began.

"They're good," Archie said, opening the box and taking out a chocolate. He inhaled its flavor and popped it into his mouth. He chewed slowly, deliberately, smacking his lips in exaggerated fashion. A second chocolate followed the first. And a third followed the second. His mouth was crammed with candy now and his throat rippled as he swallowed. "Delicious," he said. "And only two dollars a box—a bargain."

Somebody laughed. A short bark that was instantly cut off as if a needle had been lifted from a record.

"But you wouldn't know about the price, would you, Renault?"

Jerry shrugged. But his heart began to beat wildly. He knew there had to be a showdown. And this was it.

Archie reached for another chocolate. Into his mouth. "How many boxes have you sold, Renault?"

"None."

"None?" Archie's gentle voice curled in surprise and wonder. He swallowed, shaking his head in mock puzzlement. Without taking his eyes from Jerry, he called, "Hey, Porter, how many boxes have you sold?"

"Twenty-one."

"Twenty-one?" Archie's voice was now filled with awe. "Hey, Porter, you must be one of those hustling, eager-beaver freshmen, huh?"

"I'm a senior."

"A senior?" More awe. "You mean to tell me you're a big-shot senior and you've still got enough spirit left to get out there and sell all those chocolates? Beautiful, Porter." The voice full of mockery—or was it? "Anybody else here sell chocolates?"

A chorus of numbers filled the air as if The Vigil members were calling bids at a weird auction.

"Forty-two."

"Thirty-three."

"Twenty."

"Nineteen."

"Forty-five."

Archie raised his hands and silence fell. Someone in the gym fell against the wall and shouted an obscenity. Obie marveled at the way Archie ran the meetings and how The Vigils quickly took his cues. Porter hadn't sold ten boxes, if any at all. Obie himself had only sold sixteen but had called out forty-five.

"And you, Renault, a freshman, a new student who should be filled with the spirit of Trinity, you haven't sold any? Zero? Nothing?" His hand reached for another chocolate. Actually, he loved them. Not as good as Hershey with almonds but an acceptable substitute.

"That's right," Jerry said, his voice small, a wrong-end-of-the-telescope kind of voice.

"Do you mind if I ask why?"

Jerry pondered the question. What should he do? Play a game? Tell it straight? But he wasn't sure if it would make sense if he told it straight, especially to a roomful of strangers.

"It's personal," he said finally, feeling like a loser, knowing he couldn't win. It had all been going so beautifully. Football, school, a girl who had smiled at him at the bus stop. He had edged close to her and seen her name written on one of her books—Ellen Barrett. She had smiled at him two days in a row and he'd been too shy to speak to her but had looked up all the Barretts in the phone book. Five of them. Tonight he was planning to call them up, track her down. It seemed to him that he'd be able to talk to her on the phone. Now, for some reason, he had the feeling he would never talk to her, never play football again—a crazy feeling but one that he couldn't shake.

Archie had been licking his fingers, one at a time,

letting the echo of Jerry's response linger in the air. It was so quiet that he heard someone's stomach growl intimately.

"Renault," Archie said, friendly, his voice conversational. "I'll tell you something. Nothing's personal here in The Vigils. No secrets here, understand." He took a final suck at his thumb. "Hey, Johnson."

"Right," a voice called behind Jerry.

"How many times you jack off every day?"

"Twice," Johnson replied quickly.

"See?" asked Archie. "No secrets here, Renault. Nothing personal. Not in The Vigils."

Jerry had taken a shower this morning before school but now he smelled his own perspiration.

"Come on," Archie said, a good friend now, encouraging, coaxing. "You can tell us."

Carter blew air out of his mouth in exasperation. He was losing patience with Archie's cat and mouse crap. He had sat here for two years watching Archie play his silly games with kids, having Archie act the big shot as if he ran the show. Carter carried the responsibility for the assignments on his shoulders. As president, he also had to keep the other guys in line, keep them psyched up, ready to help make Archie's assignments work. And Carter wasn't crazy about this chocolate stuff. It was something beyond the control of The Vigils. It involved Brother Leon and he didn't trust Leon as far as he could throw him. Now, he watched the kid Renault, looking as if he was ready to faint with fright, his face pale and eyes wide with dread, and Archie having fun with him. Jesus. Carter hated this psychological crap. He loved boxing where everything was visible—the jabs, the hooks, the roundhouse swings, the glove in the stomach.

"Okay, Renault, play time is over," Archie said. The gentleness was gone from his voice. No chocolates in his mouth. "Tell us—why aren't you selling chocolates?"

"Because I don't want to," Jerry said, still stalling. Because—what else could he do?

"You don't want to?" Archie asked, incredulous.

Jerry nodded. He'd bought time.

"Hey, Obie."

"Right," Obie answered, stung. Why the hell did Archie have to pick on him all the time? What the hell did he want now?

"Do you want to come to school every day, Obie?"

"Hell, no," Obie responded, knowing what Archie wanted and giving it to him but resentful as well, feeling like a stooge, as if Archie was the ventriloquist and Obie the dummy.

"But you *come* to school, don't you?"

"Hell, yes."

Laughter greeted the answer and Obie allowed himself a smile. But a quick look from Archie wiped the smile away. Archie was dead serious. He could tell that by the way his lips were tight and thin and his eyes flashing like neon signs.

"See?" Archie said, swiveling back to Renault. "Everybody has to do things in this world they don't want to."

A terrific sadness swept over Jerry. As if somebody had died. The way he felt standing in the cemetery that day they buried his mother. And nothing you could do about it.

"Okay, Renault," Archie said, a finality in his voice.

You could feel the room tense. Obie sucked in his breath. Here it comes, the Archie touch.

"Here's your assignment. Tomorrow at the roll call, you take the chocolates. You say, 'Brother Leon, I accept the chocolates.'"

Stunned, Jerry blurted out "What?"

"Something wrong with your hearing, Renault?" Turning aside, he called, "Hey, McGrath, did you hear me?"

"Hell, yes."

"What did I say?"

"You said the kid should start selling chocolates."

Archie returned his attention to Jerry. "You're getting off easy, Renault. You've disobeyed The Vigils. That calls for punishment. Although The Vigils don't believe in violence, we have found it necessary to have a punishment code. The punishment is usually worse than the assignment. But we're letting you off cheap, Renault. We're just asking you to take the chocolates tomorrow. And sell them."

Jesus, Obie thought in disbelief. The great Archie Costello is running scared. The word "asking" was the tipoff. A slip of the lip, maybe. But as if Archie was trying to bargain with the kid, *asking,* for crying out loud. I've got you, Archie, you bastard. Obie had never known such sweet victory. The goddam freshman was going to screw Archie up, at last. Not the Black Box. Not Brother Leon. Not his own cleverness. But a skinny freshman. Because Obie was certain of one thing as if it was a natural law, like gravity—Renault wasn't going to sell the chocolates. He could tell by looking at the kid, standing there scared, like he could shit his pants, but not backing down. While Archie was *asking* him to sell the chocolates. Asking.

"Dismissed," Archie called out.

Carter was surprised at the sudden dismissal and he banged the gavel too hard, almost splitting the crate he used as a desk. He had a feeling that he had missed a beat somewhere, had missed a crucial moment. Archie and all his subtle crap. What the kid Renault needed was a stiff jab to the jaw and another to the belly. That'd make him sell the frigging chocolates. Archie and his stupid *let's not have any violence.* Anyway, the meeting was over and Carter felt like working out, like working up a sweat with the gloves and the big bag.

He banged the gavel again.

Chapter 26

"Hello."

His mind went blank.

"Hello?"

Was it her? But it had to be—this was the last Barrett in the book and the voice was fresh and appealing, the kind of voice that went with all that beauty he had seen at the bus stop.

"Hello," he managed, his voice emerging as an ugly croak.

"Is this Danny?" she asked.

He was instantly, insanely jealous of Danny, whoever Danny was.

"No," he croaked again, miserably.

"Who is this?" she asked, annoyance now in her voice.

"Is this Ellen? Ellen Barrett?" The name was strange on his tongue. He had never said it aloud although he had whispered it silently a thousand times.

Silence.

"Look," he began, his heart beating desperately. "Look, you don't know who I am but I see you every day . . ."

"Are you some kind of pervert?" she asked, not horrified at all but good-naturedly curious, like, "Hey ma, I've got a pervert on the line."

"No. I'm the fellow at the bus stop."

"What fellow? What bus stop?" Her voice had lost all its demureness. It had become a wise-guy, show-me kind of voice.

He wanted to say you smiled at me yesterday, the day before that, last week. And I love you. But couldn't. He suddenly saw how futile, how ridiculous the situation was. A fellow didn't call up a girl on the evidence of a smile and introduce himself this way. She probably smiled at a hundred guys a day.

"I'm sorry for bothering you," he said.

"Are you sure this isn't Danny? Are you trying to put me on, Danny? Look, Danny, I'm getting tired of you and your crap . . ."

Jerry hung up. He didn't want to hear anymore. The word "crap," echoing now in his mind, had destroyed all illusion about her. Like meeting a lovely girl and having her smile reveal rotten teeth. But his heart was still beating wildly. *Are you some kind of pervert?* Maybe I am. Not a sexual pervert but another kind. Wasn't refusing to sell the chocolates a kind of perversion? Wasn't it crazy to go on refusing to sell the chocolates, particularly after that last warning yesterday by Archie Costello and The Vigils? And yet this morning, he had stood his ground and fired a level and positive *No* at Brother Leon. For the first time, the word brought exultancy to him, a lifting of the spirit.

With the latest *No* resounding in his ears, Jerry had expected the school building to fall or something dramatic to happen. Nothing. He had seen Goober shake his head in dismay. But Goober didn't know about this new feeling, the sense that his bridges were burning behind him and for once in his life he didn't care. He was still buoyant when he arrived home, otherwise, he wouldn't have had the courage to call all those Barretts and to actually talk to the girl. It had been a miserable failure, of course. But he had made the call, taken a step, broken the routine of his days and nights.

He went into the kitchen, suddenly ravenous, and dumped some ice cream from the freezer into a dish.

"My name is Jerry Renault and I'm not going to sell the chocolates," he said to the empty apartment.

The words and his voice sounded strong and noble.

Chapter 27

They shouldn't have picked Frankie Rollo for an assignment, of course. A junior, Rollo was insolent, a troublemaker. He was a non-participant, refusing to take part in athletics or extracurricular activities that were so important in the Trinity scene. He seldom opened a book and never did any homework, but he managed to survive because he possessed a native and cunning intelligence. His major talent was cheating. He was also lucky. Under ordinary circumstances, he was the kind of guy Archie took pleasure in assigning, watching him bend or break. All these so-called rough characters melted into ninety-seven-pound weaklings when confronted by Archie and The Vigils. The scorn and the swagger evaporated as they stood ill-at-ease in the storage room. But not Frankie Rollo. He stood loose and easy, unintimidated.

"Your name?" Archie asked.

"Come on, Archie," Rollo replied, smiling at all this foolishness. "You know my name."

The silence was awesome. But before that silence, a gasp from someone in the room. Archie was careful to keep his poker face, intent on not betraying an emotion. But he was shaken inside. No one had ever reacted this way before. No one had ever challenged Archie or an assignment.

"Let's not have any crap, Rollo," growled Carter. "Let's hear your name."

A pause. Archie swore silently. It was irritating to have Carter step in that way, as if he was coming to Archie's rescue. Ordinarily, Archie ran the meetings his way, not anybody else's way.

Rollo shrugged. "My name is Frankie Rollo," he announced in sing-song fashion.

"You think you're a big shot, don't you?" Archie asked.

Rollo didn't respond but the smirk on his face was an eloquent answer.

"A big shot," Archie repeated, as if savoring the word, but stalling, playing for time, shifting his thoughts, knowing it would be necessary to improvise, to turn this insolent bastard into a victim.

"You said it, not me," Rollo said smugly.

"We like big shots here," Archie said. "In fact, that's our specialty—turning big shots into little shots."

"Cut the shit, will you, Archie?" Rollo said. "You're not impressing anybody."

Again that terrible silence, like a shock wave, stunning the room, an invisible blow. Even Obie who had looked forward to the day when a victim would defy the great Archie Costello blinked in disbelief.

"What did you say?" Archie asked, biting off every word and spitting it at Rollo.

"Hey, you guys," Rollo said, swiveling away from Archie and addressing the entire assembly. "I'm not a scared kid who pees his pants because the big bad Vigils call him to a meeting. Hell, you guys can't even scare a punk freshman into selling a few lousy chocolates . . ."

"Look, Rollo," Archie began.

But he didn't have a chance to finish as Carter leaped to his feet. Carter had been waiting for a moment like this for months, his hands itching for action in the storage room instead of sitting there week by week as Archie played his little cat-and-mouse games.

"That's enough out of you, Rollo," Carter said. Simultaneously, his hand shot out and struck Rollo on the jaw. Rollo's head snapped back—*snap* like a knuckle cracking—and he bellowed with pain. As Rollo lifted his hands to his face in tardy defense, Carter's fist sank sickeningly into his stomach. Rollo groaned and retched, doubled over, clutching himself in disbelief, gasping for breath. He was shoved from behind, and dropped to the floor coughing and spitting, crawling on all fours.

A muffled roar of approval rose from The Vigils. At last, action, physical action, something you could see with your own eyes.

"Get him out of here," Carter said.

Rollo was picked up by two Vigil members and half-carried, half-dragged toward the doorway. Archie had watched Rollo's swift demolition in dismay. He resented Carter's quick move into the spotlight, the way the guys had cheered Carter on. It had placed Archie at a disadvantage for the first time as assigner because Rollo had only been the curtain raiser, a bit of amusement Obie had arranged to enliven the proceedings. Actually, the meeting had been called to discuss Renault and what could be done about the stubborn freshman who refused to fall into line.

Carter called for order, banging his gavel on the table. In the developing silence, they could hear Rollo being dumped onto the gymnasium floor outside and then the sound of vomiting like a toilet being flushed.

"Okay, quiet," Carter demanded, as if he were yelling at Rollo to quit throwing up. Then he turned to Archie. "Sit down," he said. Archie recognized the command in Carter's voice. For a moment, he was tempted to challenge him but he realized that The Vigils had approved Carter's action against Rollo. This was no time to have a showdown with Carter, it was time to play it cool, cool. Archie sat.

"We've arrived at the moment of truth, Archie," Carter said. "And here's how I read it—tell me if I'm wrong. When a gross creep like Rollo comes in here and challenges The Vigils, then there's something wrong. Very wrong. We can't afford to have guys like Rollo thinking they can screw around with us. The word will spread and The Vigils fall apart." Carter paused to let them imagine the dissolution of The Vigils. "Now, I said that something is very wrong. And I'll tell you who's wrong. We are."

His words were greeted with surprise.

"How come *we're* wrong?" Obie, the perennial straight man, called out.

"First of all, because we let our name get connected with the goddam chocolate sale. Like it's our baby or something. Second of all, like Rollo said, we let a punk freshman make fools out of us." He turned to Archie. "Right, Archie?" The question was loaded with malice.

Archie didn't say anything. He was suddenly in a roomful of strangers and he decided to do nothing at all. When in doubt, play the waiting game. Watch for an opening. It would be ridiculous to disagree with Carter, of course. Word had been spreading throughout the school—the kid had refused to sell the chocolates in direct defiance of The Vigils. That's why they had assembled here this afternoon.

"Obie, show us what you found this morning on the bulletin board," Carter said.

Obie was eager to comply. Reaching under his chair he withdrew a poster that he had folded in two. Unfolded, the poster was about the size of an ordinary kitchen window. Obie held it up for all to see. The poster proclaimed in scrawled, scarlet letters—

SCREW THE CHOCOLATES
AND
SCREW THE VIGILS

"I saw the poster because I was late for math," Obie explained. "It was on the bulletin board in the main corridor."

"Do you think many guys saw it?" Carter asked.

"No. I'd shot by the bulletin board a minute before on the way to my locker for my math book. And the poster wasn't there. Chances are hardly anybody saw it."

"You think Renault put it up?" someone asked.

"No," Carter snorted. "Renault doesn't have to go around putting up posters. He's been saying screw The Vigils and the chocolates for weeks now. But this shows what's happening. The word is spreading. If Renault can get away with defying us, other people are gonna try." Finally, he turned to Archie. "Okay, Archie. You're the brains of the outfit. And you also got us into this mess. Where do we go from here?"

"You're pushing panic buttons for nothing," Archie said, voice quiet and casual. He knew what he must do—regain his previous status, wipe away the memory of Rollo's defiance and prove that he, Archie Costello, was still in command. He had to show them that he could take care of both Renault and the chocolates. And he was ready for them. While Carter had been making speeches and Obie flashing his poster around, Archie's mind had been racing, probing, testing. He always worked better under pressure, anyway. "First of all, you can't go around beating up half the kids in the school. That's why I usually lay off the strong-arm stuff in the assignments. The brothers would close us down in no time and the kids would really start sabotaging if we started hurting people." Noticing Carter's frown, Archie decided to throw him a bone—Carter still ran the meetings and as Vigils president he could be a dangerous adversary. "All right, Carter, I'll admit you did a beautiful job on Rollo and he had it coming. But nobody gives a damn about Rollo. He can lay in his vomit till kingdom come and nobody'd care. But Rollo's an exception."

"Rollo's an example," Carter said. "Let the word spread about Rollo and we won't have to worry about other kids acting wise or putting up posters."

Anticipating a deadlock on that topic, Archie changed directions. "But that doesn't sell chocolates, Carter," Archie said. "You told us The Vigils are linked up with the sale. Then the solution is simple. Let's get the goddam sale over with as soon as possible. Let's sell the chocolates. If Renault's turning into some kind of rebel hero because he's not selling the chocolates, how the hell is he going to look when everybody in the school is selling, except him?"

Murmurs of assent came from the members, but Carter appeared doubtful. "And how do we get everybody in the school to start selling the chocolates, Archie?"

Archie allowed himself the indulgence of a quiet, confident laugh, but closed his fists to hide his moist palms. "Simple, Carter. Like all great schemes and plans, it has the beauty of simplicity." The guys waited, spellbound as always when Archie began to outline assignments and plans. "We make selling chocolates popular. We make it cool to sell the things. We spread the word. We organize. We bring in the class officers, the homeroom officers, the student council, the kids with influence. Do or die for good old Trinity! Everybody sells!"

"Not everybody will want to sell fifty boxes,

Archie," Obie called out, disturbed because somehow Archie had taken charge again—he had them eating out of his hand.

"They will, Obie," Archie predicted, "they will. Do your thing, they say, Obie, do your thing. Well, we're going to make selling chocolates the thing to do. And The Vigils will come out on top as usual. The school will love us for it—getting rid of their chocolates. We'll be able to write our own ticket with Leon and the brothers. Why do you think I pledged support to Leon in the first place?" Archie's voice was gentle with assurance, the old gentleness they all recognized as Archie's hallmark when he was sailing high, wide and handsome. They admired the way Carter had employed his fists to demolish Rollo but they felt more secure with Archie in command, Archie who was capable of surprise after surprise.

"How about Renault?" Carter asked.

"Don't worry about Renault."

"But I do, I worry about him," Carter said, sarcastically. "He's making patsies out of us."

"The Renault thing will take care of itself," Archie said. Couldn't Carter and the others see? Were they so blind to human nature, to developing situations? "Let me put it this way, Carter. Before the sale is over, Renault will be wishing with all his heart that he had sold the chocolates. And the school will be glad he didn't."

"Okay," Carter said, banging the gavel. He always banged the gavel when he was unsure of himself. The gavel was an extension of his fist. But feeling that Archie had somehow eluded him, had somehow won a victory, Carter said, "Look, Archie, if this backfires, if the sale doesn't work, then you've screwed yourself up, do you understand? You'll be all done and it won't take the Black Box."

Blood stung Archie's cheeks and a pulse throbbed dangerously in his temple. No one had ever talked to him that way before, not in front of everyone like this. With an effort he made himself stay loose, kept that smile on his lips like a label on a bottle, hiding his humiliation.

"You'd better be right, Archie," Carter said. "As far as I'm concerned, you're on probation until the last chocolate's sold."

The final humiliation. Probation.

Archie kept that smile on his face until he felt his cheeks would crack.

Chapter 28

He handed the ball off to Guilmet, slapping it into his belly, and then hung in there, waiting for Carter to lunge through the line. The play called for Jerry to hit Carter low and send him toppling, an assignment Jerry didn't relish. Carter was easily fifty pounds heavier and he was used by the coach to keep the freshmen squad on their toes. But the coach always said, "It doesn't matter how big the body, it's what you do with it." Now, Jerry waited for Carter to emerge from the jungle of skirmishing bodies as Guilmet plunged off tackle. And there he was like a freight train on the loose, out of control, rampaging wildly, trying to careen toward Guilmet but too late, too late. Jerry leaped toward him, low, aiming for that vulnerable territory of the knees, the target pinpointed by the coach. Carter and Jerry collided like a street accident. Colored lights whirled—Fourth of July on an October afternoon. Jerry felt himself lunging toward the ground, arms and legs askew, all mixed up with Carter's arms and legs. There was exhilaration in the collision, the honest contact of football, not as beautiful maybe as a completed pass or a fake that threw your opponents off balance but beautiful nevertheless and manly, prideful.

The good damp smell of the grass, the earth, rushed into Jerry's nostrils and he let himself be carried on the waves of the sweet moment, knowing he'd carried out his assignment: get Carter. He glanced up to see Carter raising himself in astonishment, shaking his head. Jerry grinned as he got to his feet. Suddenly, he was struck from behind, a vicious blow to his kidneys, sickening in its impact. His knees caved in and he sank to the ground again. As he attempted to turn around to find out who had attacked him, another blow landed, some place, and Jerry felt himself hurtling off-balance to the ground. He felt his eyes watering, tears spilling onto his cheeks. He looked around and saw the fellows getting into position for the next play.

"Come on, Renault," the coach called.

He got to one knee, then managed to stand on both feet. The pain was subsiding, translated now into a dull spreading ache.

"Come on, come on," the coach urged, irritable as usual.

Jerry made his way tenderly toward the lineup. He thrust his head and shoulders into the huddle, considering what play he should call next, but a part of him was not concerned with the play or the game. He lifted his head and scanned the field, as if he were figuring out what to do next. Who had assaulted him that way? Who hated him so much that he'd racked him up so viciously?

Not Carter—Carter had been in full view. But who else? Anybody. It could have been anybody. From his own team, maybe.

"You okay?" somebody inquired.

Jerry plunged into the huddle again. Called his own number—a run-keep. At least if he carried the ball, he'd be in full view of everyone and not as vulnerable to a sneak attack.

"Let's go," he said, putting juice into the words, letting them all know that he was fine, great, ready for action. He found that his rib cage ached when he walked.

Lined up behind the center, Jerry raised his eyes

again, sweeping the players. Somebody was trying to wipe him out.

Give me eyes behind my head, he prayed, as he barked the signals.

The telephone rang as he inserted the key in the front door. Turning the key swiftly, he flung the door open and tossed his books on the chair in the hallway. The ringing went on unendingly, a lonely sound in the empty apartment.

Finally, he grabbed it off the wall.

"Hello."

Silence. Not even a dial tone. Then out of the silence, a faint sound, from a distance, getting closer, like someone chuckling, privately, at a secret intimate joke.

"Hello," Jerry said again.

The chuckle was louder now. An obscene phone call? Only girls got those, didn't they? Again that chuckle, more defined and louder but still somehow intimate and suggestive, a chuckle that said, I know something you don't know.

"Who is this?" Jerry asked.

And then the dial tone, like a fart in his ear.

That night at eleven o'clock the telephone rang again. Jerry figured it was his father—he was working the late shift at the drugstore.

He lifted the receiver and said hello.

No response.

No sound at all.

He wanted to hang up but something made him hold the instrument to his ear, waiting.

The chuckle again.

It was weirder than three o'clock this afternoon. The night, the darkness outside, the apartment riddled with lamplight shadows seemed more menacing. Forget it, Jerry told himself, it always seems worse at night.

"Hey, who is this?" he asked, the sound of his voice restoring normalcy.

Still the chuckle, almost evil in its quiet mockery.

"This some creep? Some flaky nut? Some stupid jerk?" Jerry asked. Draw him out, make him angry.

The chuckle turned into a hoot of derision.

Then the dial tone again.

He seldom kept anything of value in his locker. The school was notorious for "borrowers"—kids who weren't exactly thieves but walked off with anything that wasn't nailed down or locked up. No sense buying a lock—it would be busted the first day. Privacy was virtually non-existent at Trinity. Most of the kids didn't give a damn or have any respect for the rights of others. They rummaged desks, pried lockers open, sifted through books on a perennial search for loot—money, pot, books, watches, clothing—anything.

The morning after that first night phone call, Jerry opened his locker and shook his head in disbelief. His poster had been smeared with ink or some kind of blue paint. The message had been virtually obliterated. *Do I dare disturb the universe?* was now a grotesque jumble of unconnected letters. It was such a senseless, childish act of vandalism that Jerry was more awed than angered. Who'd do such a crazy thing? Looking down, he saw that his new gym sneakers had been slashed, the canvas now limp shreds, rag-like. He'd made the mistake of leaving them here overnight.

Ruining the poster was one thing, a gross act, the work of the animal—and all schools had animals, even Trinity. But there was nothing prankish about ruining the sneakers. That was deliberate, somebody sending him a message.

The telephone calls.

The attack on the football field.

Now this.

He closed the locker quickly so no one would see the damage. For some reason, he felt ashamed.

He'd been dreaming of a fire, flames eating unknown walls, and the siren sounded, and then it wasn't a siren but the telephone. Jerry scrambled from his bed. In the hallway, his father was slamming the receiver down on the hook. "Something funny's going on around here." The grandfather clock chimed twice.

Jerry didn't have to blink the sleep from his eyes. He was wide awake, chilled, the floor cold beneath his feet.

"Who was it?" he asked. Although he knew, of course.

"Nobody," his father answered, disgusted. "Same thing happened last night about this time. But it didn't wake you up. Some nut on the other end of the line, laughing away like it's the biggest joke in the world." He reached out and tousled Jerry's hair. "Go back to bed, Jerry. There are all kinds of nuts running around loose."

It was hours before Jerry fell into a strange dreamless sleep.

"Renault," Brother Andrew called.

Jerry looked up. He'd been immersed in his new art project—copying a two-story house in order to learn perspective. A simple exercise but he loved the ordered lines, the neatness, the stark beauty of planes and angles.

"Yes, Brother?"

"Your watercolor. The landscape assignment."

"Yes?" Puzzled. The watercolor which was a major project had taken a week of painstaking work, simply because Jerry was not at his best in free art. He was more at ease with formal or geometric designs where the composition was well-defined. But the watercolor would account for fifty percent of his mark this semester.

"Today's the final day for handing it in," the Brother said. "I don't find yours here."

"I put it on your desk yesterday," Jerry said.

"Yesterday?" Brother Andrew asked, as if he'd never heard of yesterday. He was a fastidious, precise man who ordinarily taught math but had been filling in for the regular art teacher.

"Yes, sir," Jerry said firmly.

Eyebrows arched, the Brother looked through the pile of drawings on the desk.

Jerry sighed quietly, in resignation. He knew that Brother Andrew wouldn't find the drawing there. He wanted to turn, to scan the faces of the kids in the class, to find that one kid who'd be gloating in satisfaction. Hey, you're getting paranoid, he told himself. Who'd sneak in here and remove your drawing? Who'd watch so close that they'd even know you submitted the drawing yesterday?

Brother Andrew looked up. "To use a cliché, Renault, we are locked on the horns of a dilemma. Your landscape is not here. Now, either I have lost it and I do not make a habit of losing landscapes . . ." the teacher paused here as if, incredibly, he expected a laugh, and incredibly, the laugh did come ". . . or your memory is faulty."

"I handed it in, Brother." Firmly. Without panic.

The teacher looked steadily into Jerry's eyes. Jerry

saw the honest doubt there. "Well, Renault, perhaps I *do* make a habit of losing landscapes, after all," he said, and Jerry felt a rush of camaraderie for the teacher. "At any rate, let me check further. Perhaps I left it in the teacher's lounge."

For some reason, this remark also provoked laughter and even the teacher joined in. It was late in the period and late in the day and everyone needed to relax, let down, take it easy. Jerry wanted to look around, to see whose eyes gleamed with triumph over the missing watercolor.

"Of course, Renault, as sympathetic as I am, if I do not find the landscape, then I must fail you this semester."

Jerry opened his locker.

The mess was still there. He hadn't torn down the poster or removed the sneakers, letting them remain there as symbols. Symbols of what? He wasn't certain. Looking wistfully at the poster, he pondered the damaged words: *Do I dare disturb the universe?*

The usual corridor pandemonium surrounded him, slammed locker doors, wild yells and whistles, pounding feet as the guys hurried to the after-school activities, football, boxing, debating.

Do I dare disturb the universe?

Yes, I do, I do. I think.

Jerry suddenly understood the poster—the solitary man on the beach standing upright and alone and unafraid, poised at the moment of making himself heard and known in the world, the universe.

Chapter 29

Beautiful.

Brian Cochran added the totals again and again, toying with them, playing with them, as if he were a juggler and they were fascinating figures of delight. He couldn't wait to report the totals to Brother Leon.

In the past few days, the volume of sales had risen staggeringly. Staggeringly was the correct word. Brian felt as if he were drunk on the statistics, the figures like liquor, making him lightheaded, giddy and dizzy.

What had happened? He wasn't certain. There was no single reason for the sudden turnabout, the surprising upswing, the unexpected rash of sales. But the proof of the change was not only here in the figures before him but everywhere in the school itself. Brian had witnessed the feverish activity and how the chocolates had suddenly become a vogue, a fad, the way hula hoops had caught on when they were kids in the first or second grade, the way demonstrations had been the big thing a few years ago. Rumors indicated that The Vigils had adopted the sale as a special crusade. And that was possible, although Brian hadn't made any inquiries—he always steered clear of The Vigils. However, he'd seen some of the more prominent Vigil members waylaying kids in the corridors, checking on their sales, whispering menacingly to those who had sold only a few boxes. Each afternoon, teams of fellows left the school, loaded down with chocolates. They piled into automobiles and drove off. Brian heard that the teams drove to various sections of town and invaded neighborhoods, ringing doorbells, banging on doors, a massive sales effort as if they were all encyclopedia salesmen on commission, for crying out loud. Brian heard reports that someone had gotten permission to solicit at one of the local factories—four guys had circulated through the place and sold three hundred boxes in a couple of hours. The feverish activity kept Brian hopping, maintaining the records and then rushing down to the big boards in the assembly to post the results. The hall had become the school's focal point. "Hey, look," a kid had yelled out during the last posting. "Jimmy Demers sold his fifty boxes."

That was the creepy aspect of the sale, the way the credit was being distributed among all the students. Brian didn't know whether this was fair or not but he didn't argue about methods—Brother Leon was interested in results and so was Brian. And yet Brian was made uncomfortable by the situation. A few minutes ago, Carter had walked into the office with a fistful of money. Brian treated Carter with utmost care—he was head of The Vigils.

"Okay, kid," Carter had said, flinging the money, bills and change, on the desk. "Here's the returns. Seventy-five boxes sold—one hundred fifty dollars. Count it."

"Right." Brian leaped to the task under Carter's watchful gaze. His fingers trembled and he cautioned himself to make no mistakes. Let it be one-fifty exactly.

"Right on the nose," Brian reported.

And then came the weird part.

"Let me see the roster," Carter said.

Brian handed over the list of names, each name with boxes beside it in which returns were noted as they arrived, corresponding to the master list on the big boards in the assembly hall. After studying the roster for a few minutes, Carter told Brian to credit various students with sales returns. Brian made the entries as Carter called them out: Huart, thirteen . . . DeLillo, nine . . . Lemoine . . . sixteen. And so on, until the entire seventy-five boxes had been distributed among seven or eight students.

"Those guys worked hard selling the chocolates," Carter said, a silly smile on his face. "I want to make sure they get credit."

"Right," Brian said, not making waves. He knew, of course, that none of the fellows chosen by Carter had sold the chocolates. But that was not his business.

"How many guys reached the fifty quota today?" Carter asked.

Brian consulted his figures. "Six, counting Huart and LeBlanc. Those sales they just made put them over the top." Brian actually was able to keep a straight face.

"Know what, Cochran? You're a bright boy. You're cool. You catch on fast."

Fast? Hell, they'd been juggling the sales all week long and Brian hadn't caught on for two entire days. He was tempted now to ask Carter if the campaign had turned into a Vigils project—like one of Archie Costello's assignments—but decided to hold down his curiosity.

Before the afternoon had ended, the sale of four hundred and seventy-five boxes had been received—cold, cold cash—as the teams returned to school with horns blowing, high with the hilarity of success.

When Brother Leon arrived, they totaled the sales together and discovered that fifteen thousand and ten boxes of chocolates had been sold thus far. Only five thousand to go—or four thousand, nine hundred and ninety to be exact, as Brother Leon pointed out in that fussy meticulous way of his. But Leon wasn't a problem today. He, too, seemed giddy, high, his wet eyes sparkling with the success of the sale.

He actually called Brian by his first name.

When Brian went to the assembly hall to post the latest figures, a cheering bunch of fellows applauded as he made the entries. No one had ever applauded Brian Cochran before and he felt like a football hero, of all things.

Chapter 30

There was no necessity for the chocolate roll call now because most of the students were bringing their returns directly to Brian Cochran in the office. But Brother Leon persisted anyway. The Goober noticed that the teacher now took a delight in the process, making a big deal of it. He read off the latest sales as reported to Brian Cochran, reciting them to the class in detail, lingering over the names and the totals, wringing as much drama and satisfaction out of the situation as possible. And he had stooges or frightened kids like David Caroni who sang out their reports in the classroom as Leon basked in the totals.

"Let's see, Hartnett," Leon said, shaking his head in pleased surprise. "The report says you sold fifteen boxes yesterday, bringing your total to forty-three. Wonderful!" And he'd glanced slyly at Jerry.

It was all ridiculous, of course, because Hartnett hadn't sold any chocolates at all. The sales had been made by the teams of fellows who went out every afternoon. The school had become chocolate crazy. But not Goober. As a show of sympathy to Jerry, he had decided to stop selling the chocolates altogether and his total had remained unchanged for the past week at twenty-seven. It was little enough to do.

"Mallan," Leon was calling out.

"Seven."

"Let me see now, Mallan. Why, that brings your total to forty-seven. Congratulations, Mallan. I'm sure you'll be selling those three remaining boxes today."

Goober shriveled in his seat. Next would be Parmentier. And then Jerry. He glanced toward Jerry, saw him sitting erect in his chair as if he was looking forward to having his name called.

"Parmentier."

"Seven."

"Parmentier, Parmentier," Leon marveled. "That makes your total, yes, by George, fifty! You've made the quota, Parmentier. Good boy, good boy! A round of cheers, gentlemen."

Goober faked his cheer—little enough.

The pause. And then Leon's voice sang out, "Renault!" That was the exact description—sang. His voice exultant, lyrical. Goober realized Leon didn't care now whether Jerry sold chocolates or not.

"No," Jerry answered, his own voice clear and forceful, ringing with a triumph of its own.

Maybe both of them could win. Maybe a showdown could be averted, after all. The sale was winding down. It could end in a stalemate and eventually be forgotten, absorbed by other school activities.

"Brother Leon."

All eyes turned to Harold Darcy who had spoken.

"Yes, Harold."

"May I ask a question?"

A frown of annoyance from the teacher. He'd been having such a great time that he resented the interruption.

"Yes, yes, Darcy."

"Would you ask Renault why he isn't selling the chocolates like everybody else?"

The sound of a car horn could be heard from two or three blocks away. Brother Leon's face was guarded. "Why do you want to know?" he asked.

"I figure it's my right to know. The right of everybody to know." He looked around for support. Somebody called out, "Right on." Darcy said, "Everybody else is doing his part, why isn't Renault?"

"Would you care to answer that, Renault?" the teacher said, the moist eyes flashing, the malice unmistakable.

Jerry paused, face flushed. "It's a free country," he said, words which touched off a ripple of laughter. Someone snickered. Brother Leon looked positively joyous and Goober felt nauseous.

"I'm afraid you'll have to be more original than that, Renault," Brother Leon said, playing to his audience, as usual.

Goober could see the color rising to Jerry's cheeks. He was also aware of a change in the class, a subtle alteration of mood and atmosphere. Until this particular roll call, the class had been neutral, indifferent toward Jerry's position, maintaining a live-and-let-live attitude. Today however, the air was filled with resentment. More than resentment—hostility. Take Harold Darcy. Ordinarily he was a regular kid, minding his own business with no tinge of the crusader or fanatic about him. And suddenly here he was challenging Jerry.

"Did you say this sale was voluntary, Brother Leon?" Jerry asked.

"Yes," the teacher said, hanging back as if he were trying to fade into the background, letting Jerry betray himself with his own words.

"Then I don't feel that I have to sell the chocolates."

A ripple of resentment across the classroom.

"You think you're better than we are?" Darcy shot out.

"No."

"Then who do you think you are?" Phil Beauvais asked.

"I'm Jerry Renault and I'm not going to sell the chocolates."

Damn it, Goober thought. Why didn't he bend a little? Just a little.

The bell rang. For a moment, the boys sat there, waiting, knowing that the issue hadn't been settled, something ominous in the waiting. Then the moment broke and the boys began to push back their chairs, rising from the desks, shuffling as usual. No one looked at Jerry Renault. By the time Goober got to the door, Jerry was walking swiftly to his next class. A crowd of boys, Harold Darcy among them, stood sullenly in the corridor, watching Jerry's progress down the hallway.

Later that afternoon, The Goober wandered to the assembly hall, attracted by cheers and hoots. He stood in the rear of the hall, watching as Brian Cochran posted the latest returns. There were probably fifty or sixty guys in the place, unusual for that time of day. Every time Cochran wrote in new sales, the fellows burst forth in cheers, led by, of all people, big bruising Carter who probably hadn't sold any chocolates at all but had others do his dirty work.

Brian Cochran consulted a sheet of paper he held in his hand and then went to one of the three big boards. Beside the name Roland Goubert, he wrote down the number fifty.

For a moment, it didn't occur to The Goober who Roland Goubert was—he watched, fascinated, unbelieving. And then—hey, that's me!

"Goober sold his fifty boxes," someone called.

Cheers, applause and ear-splitting whistles.

The Goober started to step forward in protest. He had only sold twenty-seven boxes, damn it. He had stopped at twenty-seven to show that he was supporting Jerry, even though nobody knew, not even Jerry. And now the whole thing evaporated and he found himself sinking back in the shadows, as if he could shrivel into invisibility. He didn't want trouble. He'd had enough trouble, and he had held on. But he knew his days at Trinity would be numbered if he walked into that group of jubilant guys and told them to erase the fifty beside his name.

Out in the corridor, The Goober's breath came fast. But otherwise he felt nothing. He willed himself to feel nothing. He didn't feel rotten. He didn't feel like a traitor. He didn't feel small and cowardly. And if he didn't feel all these things, then why was he crying all the way to his locker?

Chapter 31

"What's your hurry, kid?"

It was a familiar voice—the voice of all the bullies in the world, Harvey Cranch who used to wait for Jerry outside the third grade at St. John's, and Eddie Herman at summer camp who delighted in the small tortures he inflicted on the younger kids and the complete stranger who knocked him down at the circus one summer and tore the ticket from his hand. That was the voice he heard now: the voice of all the bullies and troublemakers and wise guys in the world. Mocking, goading, cajoling and looking for trouble. *What's your hurry, kid?* The voice of the enemy.

Jerry looked at him. The kid stood before him in defiant posture, feet planted firmly on the ground, legs spread slightly apart, hands flat against the sides of his legs as if he wore two-gun holsters and was ready to draw, or as if he was a karate expert with hands waiting to chop and slice. Jerry didn't know a thing about karate, except in his wildest dreams when he demolished his foes without mercy.

"I asked you a question," the kid said.

Jerry recognized him now—a wise guy named Janza. A freshman-baiter, somebody to stay away from.

"I know you asked me a question," Jerry said, sighing. He knew what was coming.

"What question?"

And there it was. The taunt, the beginning of the old cat-and-mouse game.

"The question you asked me," Jerry countered but knowing the futility of it. It didn't matter what he said or how he said it. Janza was looking for an opening and he'd find it.

"And what was it?"

"You wanted to know what was my hurry."

Janza smiled, having won his point, gained his little victory. A smug superior smile spread across his face, a knowing smile, as if he knew all of Jerry's secrets, a lot of dirty things about him.

"Know what?" Janza asked.

Jerry waited.

"You look like a wise guy," Janza said.

Why did the wise guys always accuse other people of being wise guys?

"What makes you think I'm a wise guy?" Jerry asked, trying to stall, hoping someone would come along. He remembered how Mr. Phaneuf had rescued him once when Harvey Cranch had cornered him near the old man's barn. But there was nobody around now. The football practice had been miserable. He hadn't completed a pass and the coach had finally dismissed him. *This ain't your day, Renault, take an early shower.* Turning away from the coach, Jerry had seen the secret smirks, the quick smiles on the faces of the players and had realized the truth. They'd dropped his passes purposely, had refused to block. Now that Goober had quit the team, there was no one he could trust. More paranoia, he chided himself, trudging along the pathway that led from the football field to the gym. And had encountered Janza who should have been out there practicing but had been waiting for him.

"Why do I think you're a wise guy?" Janza asked now. "Because you put on a big act, kid. You try to get by with a sincerity act. But you're not kidding me. You live in the closet." Janza smiled, a knowing, this-is-just-between-us smile, intimate, creepy.

"What do you mean—closet?"

Janza laughed, delighted, and touched Jerry's cheek with his hand, a brief light touch, as if they were old friends engaged in friendly conversation on an October afternoon, leaves whirling around them like giant confetti as the wind rose. Jerry figured he knew the meaning of Janza's light tap—Janza was aching for action, contact, violence. And he was getting impatient. But he didn't want to start the fight himself. He wanted to provoke Jerry into beginning— that's the way bullies worked so they could be held blameless after the slaughter. *He started it,* they'd claim. Strangely enough, Jerry felt as though he could actually beat Janza in a fight. He could feel a gathering of outrage that promised strength and endurance. But he didn't want to fight. He didn't want to return to grammar school violence, the cherished honor of the schoolyard that wasn't honor at all, the necessity of proving yourself by bloody noses and black eyes and broken teeth. Mainly, he didn't want to fight for the same reason he wasn't selling the chocolates—he wanted to make his own decisions, do his own thing, like they said.

"This is what I mean by *closet,*" Janza said, his hand flicking out again, touching Jerry's cheek, but lingering this time for the fraction of a second in faint caress. "That you're hiding in there."

"Hiding what? Hiding from who?"

"From everybody. From yourself, even. Hiding that deep dark secret."

"What secret?" Confused now.

"That you're a fairy. A queer. Living in the closet, hiding away."

Vomit threatened Jerry's throat, a nauseous geyser he could barely hold down.

"Hey, you're blushing," Janza said. "The fairy's blushing . . ."

"Listen . . ." Jerry began but not knowing, really, how to begin or where. The worst thing in the world—to be called queer.

"*You* listen," Janza said, cool now, knowing he had struck a vulnerable spot. "You're polluting Trinity. You won't sell the chocolates like everybody else and now we find out you're a fairy." He shook his head in mock, exaggerated admiration. "You're really something, know that? Trinity has tests and ways of weeding the homos out but you were smart enough to get by, weren't you? You must be creaming all over— wow, four hundred ripe young bodies to rub against . . ."

"I'm not a fairy," Jerry cried.

"Kiss me," Janza said, puckering his lips grotesquely.

"You son of a bitch," Jerry said.

The words hung on the air, verbal flags of battle. And Janza smiled, a radiant smile of triumph. This is what he'd wanted all along, of course. This had been the reason for the encounter, the insults.

"What did you call me?" Janza asked.

"A son of a bitch," Jerry said, measuring out the words, saying them deliberately, eager now for the fight.

Janza threw back his head and laughed. The laughter surprised Jerry—he'd expected retaliation. Instead, Janza stood there utterly relaxed, hands on his hips, amused.

And that was when Jerry saw them. Three or four of them emerging from bushes and shrubbery, running, crouched, keeping themselves low. They were small, pigmy-like, and they moved so swiftly toward him that he couldn't get a good look at them, saw only a smear of smiling faces, smiling evilly. More coming now, five or six others, slipping into view from behind a cluster of pine trees, and before Jerry could gird himself for a fight or even raise his arms in defense, they were swarming all over him, hitting him high and low, tumbling him to the ground as if he was some kind of helpless Gulliver. A dozen fists pummeled his body, fingernails tore at his cheek and a finger clawed at his eye. They wanted to blind him. They wanted to kill him. Pain arrowed in his groin— somebody had kicked him there. The blows rained upon him without mercy, with no let-up, and he tried to curl up and make himself small, hiding his face but somebody was pounding his head furiously, *stop, stop,* another kick in his groin and he couldn't hold down the vomit now, it was coming and he tried to open his mouth to let it spray forth. As he threw up, they let him go, someone yelled "Jesus" in disgust and they withdrew. He could hear their gasps, their running feet receding although somebody stayed behind to kick him again, this time in his lower back, the final sheet of pain that drew a black curtain over his eyes.

Chapter 32

Sweet, sweet in the dark, safe. Dark and safe and quiet. He dared not move. He was afraid that his body would come loose, all his bones spilling out like a building collapsing, like a picket fence clattering apart. A small sound reached his ears and he realized it was himself, crooning softly, as if he were singing himself a lullaby. Suddenly, he missed his mother. Her absence formed tears on his cheeks. He hadn't cried at all from the beating, had lain there on the ground for a few moments after the brief blackout, and then had dragged himself up and made it agonizingly to the locker room at school, walking as if on a tightrope and one misstep would send him hurtling into depths below: oblivion. He'd washed himself, cold water like liquid fingernails inflaming the scratches on his face. I won't sell their chocolates whether they beat me up or not. And I'm not a fairy, not a queer. He had stolen away from the school, not wanting anyone to witness his painful passage down the street to the bus stop. He kept his collar up, like a criminal, like those men in newscasts being herded into court. Funny, somebody does violence to you but you're the one who has to hide, as if you're the criminal. He shuffled to the back of the bus, grateful that it wasn't one of the crowded school buses but a maverick bus that appeared at odd hours. The bus was full of old people, old women with blue hair and big handbags and they pretended not to see him, sailing their eyes askew from him as he stalked to the rear of the bus, but their noses wrinkled as they caught the smell of vomit when he passed.

Somehow, he'd made it home on the jolting bus, made it to this quiet room where he now sat, sun bleeding low in the sky and spurting its veins on the den window. Dusk moved in. After a while, he took a warm bath, soaking in the water. Then he sat in the dark, quiet, letting himself mend, not stirring, feeling a dull ache settle in his bones now that the first waves of pain had moved away. The clock struck six. He was glad that his father was on the evening shift, at work until eleven. He didn't want his father to see him with these fresh cuts on his face, the bruises. Make it to the bedroom, he urged himself, undress, curl into cool sheets, tell him I came home sick, must be a virus, twenty-four hour flu, and keep my face hidden.

The telephone rang.

Oh no, he protested.

Let me alone.

The ringing continued, mocking him the way Janza had mocked him.

Let it be, let it be, like the Beatles sang.

Still ringing.

And he saw suddenly that he must answer. They didn't want him to answer this time. They wanted to think that he was incapacitated, injured, unable to make it to the phone.

Jerry lifted himself from the bed, surprised at his mobility, and made his way through the living room to the phone. Don't stop ringing now, he said, don't stop ringing. I want to show them.

"Hello." Forcing strength into his voice.

Silence.

"I'm here," he said, shouting the words.

Silence again. Then the lewd chuckle. And the dial tone.

"Jerry . . . oh Jerry . . ."

"Yoo hoo, Jerree . . ."

The apartment Jerry and his father occupied was three floors above street level and the voices calling Jerry's name reached him faintly, barely penetrating the closed windows. That distant quality also gave the voices a ghostly resonance, like someone calling from the grave. In fact, he hadn't been certain at first that his name was being called. Slouched at the kitchen table, forcing himself to sip Campbell's Chicken Broth, he heard the voices and thought they were the sound of kids playing in the street. Then he heard distinctly—

"Hey, Jerry . . ."

"Whatcha doing, Jerry?"

"Come on out and play, Jerry."

Ghostly voices from the past recalling when he was a little boy and the kids in the neighborhood came to the back door after supper calling him to go out and play. That was in the sweet time when he and his parents lived together in the house with the big backyard and a front lawn his father never got tired of mowing and watering.

"Hey, Jerry . . ."

But these voices calling now were not friendly after-supper voices but nighttime voices, taunting and teasing and threatening.

Jerry went into the living room and looked down cautiously, careful not to be seen. The street was deserted except for a couple of parked cars. And still the voices sang.

"Jerree . . ."

"Come out and play, Jerry . . ."

A parody of those long ago childhood pleadings.

Peering out again, Jerry saw a shooting star in

reverse. It split the darkness and he heard the dull plunk as a stone, not a star at all, hit the wall of the building near the window.

"Yoo hoo, Jerree . . ."

He squinted at the street below but the boys were well hidden. Then he saw a spray of light sweeping the trees and shrubs across the street. A pale face flared in the darkness as the ray of a flashlight caught and held it for a moment. The face disappeared in the night. Jerry recognized the plodding gait of the building custodian who evidently had been drawn out of his basement apartment by the voices. His flashlight swept the street.

"Who's there?" he shouted. "I'm gonna get the police . . ."

"Bye, bye, Jerry," a voice called.

"See you later, Jerry." Fading into the dark.

The telephone ruptured the night. Jerry groped upward from sleep, reaching for the sound. Instantly awake, he glanced at the alarm clock's luminous face. Two-thirty.

Painfully, his muscles and bones protesting, he lifted himself from the mattress and poised, on one elbow, to thrust himself from the bed.

The ringing persisted, ridiculously loud in the stillness of the night. Jerry's feet touched the floor and he padded toward the sound.

But his father was already at the phone. He glanced toward Jerry and Jerry drew back into the shadows, keeping his face hidden.

"Madmen loose in the world," his father muttered, standing there with his hand on the phone. "If you let it ring, they get their kicks. If you answer, they hang up and still get their kicks. And then start all over again."

The harassment had taken toll on his father's face, his hair disheveled, purple crescents under his eyes.

"Take the phone off the hook, Dad."

His father sighed, nodded assent. "That's giving in to them, Jerry. But what the hell. Who are *them*, anyway?" His father lifted the receiver, holding it to his ear for a moment, then turned to Jerry. "The same thing, that crazy laugh and then the dial tone." He placed the receiver on the table. "I'll report it to the telephone company in the morning." Peering in at Jerry, he said, "You okay, Jerry?"

"Fine. I'm just fine, Dad."

His father rubbed his eyes, wearily.

"Get some sleep, Jerry. A football player needs his sleep." Trying to keep it light.

"Right, Dad."

Compassion for his father welled in Jerry. Should he tell his father what it was all about? But he didn't want to involve him. His father had given in, taken the receiver off the hook, and that was defeat enough. He didn't want him to risk more.

In bed once more, small in the dark, Jerry willed his body to loosen, to relax. After a while, sleep plucked at him with soft fingers, soothing away the ache. But the phone rang in his dreams all night long.

Chapter 33

"Janza, can't you do anything right?"

"What the hell are you talking about? By the time we got through with him, he'd been willing to sell a million boxes of chocolates."

"I mean those kids. I didn't tell you to make it a gang bang."

"That was a stroke of genius, Archie. That's what I thought it was. Let him get beat up by a bunch of kids. Psychological—isn't that what you're always talking about?"

"Where'd you get them? I don't want outsiders involved in this."

"Some animals from my neighborhood. They'd beat up their own grandmothers for a quarter."

"Did you use the queer pitch on him?"

"You were right, Archie. You called it beautiful. That really spaced him out. Hey, Archie, he isn't queer, is he?"

"Of course not. That's why he blew up. If you want to get under a guy's skin, accuse him of being something he isn't. Otherwise, you're only telling him something he knows."

The silence on the phone indicated Emile's appreciation of Archie's genius.

"What's next, Archie?"

"Let's cool it, Emile. I want to keep you in reserve. We've got some other stuff going now."

"I was just starting to enjoy myself."

"You'll have other chances, Emile."

"Hey Archie."

"Yes, Emile."

"How about the picture?"

"Suppose I told you there was no picture, Emile? That there was no film in the camera that day . . ."

Wow, that Archie. Full of surprises. But was he kidding around? Or telling the truth?

"I don't know, Archie."

"Emile, stick with me. All the way. And you can't go wrong. We need men like you."

Emile swelled with pride. Was Archie talking about The Vigils? And was there really no photograph after all? What a relief that would be!

"You can count on me, Archie."

"I know that, Emile."

But after he'd hung up, Emile thought: Archie, that bastard.

Chapter 34

Suddenly, he was invisible, without body, without structure, a ghost passing transparently through the hours. He'd made the discovery on the bus going to school. Eyes avoiding his. Looking away. Kids giving him wide berth. Ignoring him, as if he wasn't there. And he realized that he really wasn't there, as far as they were concerned. It was as if he were the carrier of a terrible disease and nobody wanted to become contaminated. And so they rendered him invisible, eliminating him from their presence. All the way to school he sat alone, his wounded cheek pressed against the cool glass of the window.

The chill of morning hurried him up the walk to the school entrance. He spotted Tony Santucci. Purely from instinct, Jerry nodded hello. Tony's face was usually a mirror, reflecting back whatever greeted him—a smile for a smile, a frown for a frown. But now he stared at Jerry. Not really stared. Actually, he wasn't looking at Jerry but *through* him as if Jerry were a window, a doorway. And then Tony Santucci fled the scene, into the school.

Jerry's progress through the corridor was like the parting of the Red Sea. Nobody brushed against him. Guys stepped out of his path, giving him passage, as if reacting to some secret signal. Jerry felt as though he could walk through a wall and emerge untouched on the other side.

He opened his locker—the mess was gone. The desecrated poster had been removed and the wall scrubbed clean. The sneakers were gone. The locker had an air of absence, of being unoccupied. He thought, maybe I should look in a mirror, see if I'm still here. But he was still here, all right. His cheek still stung with pain. Staring at the inside of the locker, like looking into an upright coffin, he felt as though someone was trying to obliterate him, remove all traces of his existence, his presence in the school. Or was he becoming paranoid?

In the classrooms, the teachers also seemed to be part of the conspiracy. They let their eyes slide over him, looking elsewhere when Jerry tried to catch their attention. Once, he waved his hand frantically to answer a question but the teacher ignored him. And yet it was hard to tell about teachers—they were mysterious, they could sense when something unusual was going on. Like today. The kids are giving Renault the freeze so let's go along with it.

Resigning himself to the freeze, Jerry drifted through the day. After a while, he began to enjoy his invisibility. He was able to relax. There was no longer any need to be on his guard, or afraid of being attacked. He was tired of being afraid, tired of being intimidated.

Between classes, Jerry searched for The Goober but didn't find him. Goober would have established reality once again, planted Jerry solidly in the world once more. But Goober was absent from school and Jerry figured it was just as well. He didn't want anybody else getting involved in his trouble. It was enough that the phone calls had involved his father. He thought of his father standing at the phone last night, haunted by the persistent ringing, and he thought, I should have sold the chocolates, after all. He didn't want his father's universe to be disturbed and he wanted his own to be put in order again.

After the last class that morning, Jerry walked

freely down the corridor, headed for the cafeteria, swinging along with the crowd, enjoying his absence of identity. Approaching the stairs, he felt himself pushed from behind and he pitched forward, off balance. He began to fall, the stairs slanting dangerously before him. Somehow, he managed to grab the railing. He held on, pressing his body against the wall. As the stream of guys thudded past, he heard someone snicker, someone else hiss.

He knew he wasn't invisible any longer.

Brother Leon entered the office at the moment Brian Cochran finished his final tabulation. The end. The last total of them all. He looked up at the teacher, delighted with the timing of his arrival.

"Brother Leon, it's all over," Brian announced, triumph in his voice.

The teacher blinked rapidly, his face like a cash register that wasn't working. "Over?"

"The sale." Brian slapped down the sheet of paper. "Finished. Done with."

Brian watched the information sinking in. Leon took a deep breath and lowered himself into his chair. For an instant, Brian observed relief sweeping the teacher's face, as if a huge burden had been lifted from him. But it was only a brief glimpse. He looked at Brian sharply. "Are you sure?" he asked.

"Positive. And listen, Brother Leon. The money—it's amazing. Ninety-eight per cent has been turned in."

Leon stood up. "Let's check the figures," he said.

Anger surged through Brian. Couldn't the teacher let down for one minute? Couldn't he say "good job"? or "thank God"? Or something? Instead, "let's check the figures."

Leon's rancid breath—didn't he ever eat anything

else but bacon, for crissakes—filled the air as he stood beside Brian looking over the tabulations.

"There's only one thing," Brian said, hesitating to bring the subject up.

Leon caught the boy's doubt. "What's the matter?" he asked, more angry than curious, as if he anticipated an error on Brian's part.

"It's the freshman, Brother Leon."

"Renault? What about him?"

"Well, he still hasn't sold his chocolates. And it's weird, really weird."

"What's so weird about it, Cochran? The boy's obviously a misfit. He tried in his small ineffectual way to damage the sale and he succeeded in doing the opposite. The school rallied against him."

"But it's still weird. Our sales total comes to exactly nineteen thousand, nine hundred fifty boxes. Right on the nose. And that's practically impossible. I mean, there's always some spoilage, some boxes get lost or stolen. It's impossible to account for every single box. But this comes out right on the dot. With exactly fifty boxes missing—Renault's fifty."

"If Renault didn't sell them, then obviously they are not sold. And that's why there are fifty missing boxes," Leon said, his voice slow and reasonable, as if Brian were five years old.

Brian realized that Brother Leon didn't want to see the truth. He was only interested in the results of the sale, knowing that his previous nineteen thousand, nine hundred fifty boxes had been sold and he was off the hook. He'd probably be promoted, become Headmaster. Brian was glad he wouldn't be here next year, particularly if Leon became permanent Headmaster.

"You see what's important here, Cochran?" Leon asked, assuming his classroom voice. "School spirit.

We have disproven a law of nature—one rotten apple does not spoil the barrel. Not if we have determination, a noble cause, a spirit of brotherhood . . ."

Brian sighed, looking down at his fingers, tuning Leon out, letting the words fall meaninglessly on his ears. He thought of Renault, that strange stubborn kid. Was Leon right, after all? That the school was more important than any one kid? But weren't individuals important, too? He thought of Renault standing alone against the school, The Vigils, everybody.

Ah, the hell with it, Brian thought as Leon's voice droned on sanctimoniously. The sale was over and his job as treasurer was over. He wouldn't be involved with Leon or Archie or even Renault anymore. Thank God for little favors.

"You got the fifty boxes set aside, Obie?"

"Yes, Archie."

"Beautiful."

"What's it all about, Archie?"

"We're having an assembly, Obie. Tomorrow night. A special assembly. To report on the chocolate sale. At the athletic field."

"Why the athletic field, Archie? Why not the school?"

"Because this assembly is strictly for the student body, Obie. The brothers are not involved. But everybody else will be there."

"Everybody?"

"Everybody."

"Renault?"

"He'll be there, Obie, he'll be there."

"You're really something else, Archie, you know that?"

"I know that, Obie."

"Pardon me for asking, Archie . . ."

"Ask away, Obie."

"What do you want Renault there for?"

"To give him a chance. A chance to get rid of his chocolates, old buddy."

"I'm not your old buddy, Archie."

"I know that, Obie."

"And how's Renault going to get rid of his chocolates, Archie?"

"He's going to raffle them off."

"A raffle?"

"A raffle, Obie."

Chapter 35

A raffle, for crying out loud.

But what a raffle!

A raffle like no other in Trinity's history, in any school's history.

Archie, the architect of the event, watched the proceedings—the stadium filling up, the kids streaming in, the slips of paper being sold, passed back and forth, the lights dispelling some of the cool of the autumn evening. He stood near the improvised stage that Carter and The Vigils had erected that afternoon under Archie's direction—an old boxing ring resurrected from the bowels of the bleachers and restored to its former use except for the absence of ropes. The platform stood directly at the fifty-yard line close to the stands so that each kid would see everything and wouldn't miss any of the action. That was Archie. Give them their money's worth.

The athletic field was at least a quarter of a mile from the school and the residence where the brothers lived. But Archie had taken no chances. He had disguised the event as a football rally, strictly for students, without the inhibition of the teachers being present. They had arranged for the sweet-faced kid, Caroni, to ask for permission—Caroni who looked like a choir boy. What teacher could refuse him? And now the moment was at hand, the kids arriving, the air crisp and cool, excitement shivering through the crowd—and Renault and Janza there in the ring, glancing uneasily at each other.

Archie always marveled at things like this, things he had arranged and manipulated. For instance, all these guys tonight would be doing something else except for Archie who had been able to alter their actions. And all it took was a little bit of Archie's imagination and two phone calls.

The first call had been to Renault, the second to Janza. But Janza's call had been simply routine. Archie knew he could shape Janza's actions the way he could shape a piece of clay. But the call to Renault had required the right moves, resourcefulness and a little touch of Archie in the night. Shakespeare yet, Archie chuckled.

The phone must have rung, oh, fifty times and Archie hadn't blamed the kid for not rushing to lift the receiver. But persistence paid off and finally there was Renault on the line, the quiet *hello,* the calm voice but something else, something else. Archie had detected another quality in the voice—a deadly calm, determination. Beautiful. The kid was ready. Archie had soared with triumph. The kid wanted to come out and fight. He wanted action.

"Want to get even, Renault?" Archie goaded. "Strike back? Get revenge? Show them what you think of their goddam chocolates?"

"How do I do that?" The voice was guarded but interested. Definitely interested.

"Easy, easy," Archie responded, "if you're not chicken, that is." The needle, always the needle.

Renault was silent.

"There's a guy named Janza. He's really a rotten kid, no class at all. He's not much more than an animal. And word has gotten around that he needed the help of a bunch of kids to make you fall in line. So I figure we ought to settle the matter. At an assembly at the athletic field. Boxing gloves. Everything under control. Here's a way to get even with everybody, Renault."

"With you too, Archie?"

"Me?" The voice innocent and sweet. "Hell, why me? I was only carrying out my job. I gave you an assignment—don't sell the chocolates—and then I gave you another—sell them. You did the rest, kid. I didn't beat you up. I don't believe in violence. But you touched off the fireworks . . ."

Silence on the line again. Archie pressed on, softening his voice, cajoling, leading him on. "Look, kid, I'm giving you this choice because I believe in fair play. Here's a chance to end it all and get on with other things. Christ, there's more to life than a lousy chocolate sale. You and Janza alone in the ring, facing each other fair and square. And that's it, finished, the end, all done. I guarantee it. Archie guarantees it."

And the kid had fallen for it, hook, line and sinker, although the conversation had gone back and forth for a while. Archie had been patient. Patience always paid off. And he had won, of course.

Now, surveying his handiwork, the crowded bleachers, the frantic comings and goings as the raffle tickets were bought and sold and the directions scrawled on the tickets. Archie exulted quietly. He had successfully conned Renault and Leon and The Vigils and the whole damn school. I can con anybody. I am Archie.

Pretend you're a spotlight, Obie told himself, a spotlight sweeping the place, stopping here and there, and lingering at other places, picking up the highlights of the thing, this momentous occasion. Because, let's admit it, this *is* an important event and Archie, that bastard, that clever, clever bastard, has done it again.

Look at him down there near the fight ring, like he's king of all he surveys. And he is, of course. He's got Renault there, pale and tense as if he's facing a firing squad, and Janza, the animal, a chained animal waiting to spring loose.

Obie, the spotlight, concentrated on Renault. Poor dumb doomed kid. He can't win and he doesn't know it. Not from Archie. Nobody wins from Archie. Archie, who'd been going down to defeat—what a great scene that had been, the last Vigils meeting when he'd stood there humiliated—but now he was on top again, all the chocolates sold, in charge once more, the entire school in the palm of his hand. All of which proves that the meek don't inherit the earth. Not very original. Archie must have said it at one time or another.

Don't move. Not a muscle. Just wait. Wait it out, wait and see.

Jerry's left leg had fallen asleep.

How can your leg fall asleep when you're standing up?

I don't know. But it's asleep.

Nerves, maybe. Tension.

At any rate, small darts stung his legs and he had to fight to keep from moving. He didn't dare move, afraid he would fall apart if he moved.

He knew now that it had been a mistake coming here, that Archie had faked him out, tricked him. For a few moments while Archie's voice whispered enticingly of sweet revenge, suggesting the fight as a way of ending it all, Jerry had actually believed it was possible, possible to beat Janza and the school and even Archie. He had thought of his father and the terrible look of defeat when he had listened on the phone the other night and finally placed the receiver on the table, giving up. I'm not giving up, Jerry had pledged, listening to Archie's goading voice. He also ached for a chance to confront Janza. Janza who had called him a fairy.

So, he had agreed to meet Janza in a fight and already Archie had doublecrossed him. Had doublecrossed Janza as well. He'd allowed them to be led onto the platform, stripped to the waist, shivering slightly in the evening air, given boxing gloves. And then Archie, his eyes sparkling with triumph and malice, had explained the rules. Those rules!

Jerry had been about to protest when Janza opened his mouth. "It's okay with me. I can beat this kid any way you want."

And Jerry saw, to his dismay, that Archie had counted on Janza's reaction, had counted on the guys filing into the stadium. He had known that Jerry couldn't back away now—he had come too far. Archie had bestowed one of his sickly sweet smiles on Jerry. "What do you say, Renault? Do you accept the rules?"

What could he say? After the phone calls and the beating. After the desecration of his locker. The silent treatment. Pushed downstairs. What they did to Goober, to Brother Eugene. What guys like Archie and Janza did to the school. What they would do to the world when they left Trinity.

Jerry tightened his body in determination. At least this was his chance to strike back, to hit out. Despite the odds Archie had set up with the raffle tickets.

"Okay," Jerry had said.

Now, standing here, one leg half asleep, nausea threatening his stomach, the night chilling his flesh, Jerry wondered if he hadn't lost the moment he had said *okay.*

The raffle tickets were selling like dirty pictures.

Brian Cochran was amazed but he shouldn't have been—he was getting used to being amazed where Archie Costello was concerned. First the chocolate sale. And now this—this wacky raffle. Never anything like it at Trinity. Or anywhere. And he had to admit that he was kind of enjoying himself even though he had protested when Archie approached him this afternoon, asking him to take charge of the raffle. "You did great with the chocolates," Archie said. The compliment melted Brian's opposition. Besides, he was scared stiff of Archie and The Vigils. Personal survival, that's what Brian believed in.

He had been seized by doubt again when Archie explained how the fight and the raffle would work. How are you going to get Renault and Janza to do it? That's what Brian wanted to know. Easy, Archie assured him. Renault's looking for revenge and Janza's a beast. And they can't back down with the whole school looking on. Then Archie's voice had gone cold again and Brian had shriveled inside. "You just do your job, Cochran, sell the tickets. And leave the details to me." So Brian had lined up a bunch of kids to do the selling. And Archie had been right, of course, because there they were, Renault and Janza up there on the platform, and the tickets were selling like there was no tomorrow.

Emile Janza was tired of being treated like one of the bad guys. That's the way Archie made him feel. "Hey, animal," Archie would say. Emile wasn't an animal. He had feelings like everybody else. Like the guy in the Shakespeare thing in English I, "Cut me, do I not bleed?" All right, so he liked to screw around a little, get under people's skin. That was human nature, wasn't it? A guy had to protect himself at all times. Get them before they get you. Keep people guessing—and afraid. Like Archie with his rotten picture that didn't even exist. Archie had convinced him that there was no picture, after all. How could there be a picture, Emile, Archie'd reasoned. Remember how dim it was in the john that day? And I didn't have a flash. And there wasn't any film in the camera. And if there had been, I didn't have time to focus. The truth had both relieved Emile and made him mad as hell. But Archie had pointed out that Emile should be mad at people like Renault. Hell, Emile, guys like Renault are your enemy, not guys like me. They're the squares, Emile, they're the ones who screw it up for us, who blow the whistle, who make the rules. Then Archie had provided the climax, the door-slammer—besides, the guys are starting to talk about how Renault was beaten up, how you needed the help of others and couldn't do it yourself . . .

Emile looked across the stage at Renault. He longed for combat. To prove himself in front of the whole school. The hell with that psychology crap Archie had made him use—telling Renault he was a fairy. He should have used his fists, not his mouth.

He was impatient to get started. To wreck Renault in front of everybody, no matter what was written down on the raffle tickets.

And in a corner of his mind, there still lurked the doubt—did Archie have that picture of him in the john, after all?

Chapter 36

Those raffle tickets.

Wow! Terrific!

Archie hadn't seen any that had been filled out yet and he stopped one of the guys who'd been recruited as a salesman by Brian Cochran.

"Let's see," Archie said, holding out his hand.

The kid was quick to comply and Archie was pleased at his submissiveness. I am Archie. My wish becomes command.

The sound of the restless audience in his ears, Archie scrutinized the paper. Scrawled there, the words

Janza
Right To Jaw
Jimmy Demers

That was the simple, stunning beauty of the raffle, the unexpected twist that Archie Costello was famous for, what they always knew Archie could do—top himself. In one stroke, Archie had forced Renault to show up here, to become part of the chocolate sale, and he also placed Renault at the mercy of the school, the students. The fighters on the platform would have no will of their own. They would have to fight the way the guys in the bleachers directed them. Everybody who bought a ticket—and who could refuse?—had a chance to be involved in the fight, to watch two guys battering each other while they were at a safe distance, with no danger of getting hurt. The risky part had been getting Renault here tonight. Once he was on the platform Archie knew he could not refuse to go on, even when he heard about the tickets. And that's the way it worked out. Beautiful.

Carter approached. "They're really selling, Archie," he said. Carter appreciated the fight concept. He loved boxing. He had, in fact, bought two tickets and had gotten a kick out of deciding which blows he would call for. He'd finally decided on a right cross to the jaw and an uppercut. At the last moment, he'd almost assigned the blows to Renault—give the kid a break. But Obie was standing nearby, Obie who stuck his nose in everybody else's business. So Carter had written in Janza's name. Janza, the beast, always ready to jump when Archie said jump.

"Looks like a beautiful night," Archie said now, smugly, that know-it-all attitude Carter hated. "You see, Carter, I told you everybody was pushing panic buttons for nothing."

"I don't know how you do it, Archie," Carter was forced to admit.

"Simple, Carter, simple." Archie reveled in the moment, basking in Carter's admiration, Carter who had humiliated him at The Vigils meeting. Someday he'd get even with Carter but at the moment it was satisfying enough to have Carter regarding him with awe and envy. "You see, Carter, people are two things: greedy and cruel. So we have a perfect set-up here. The greed part—a kid pays a buck for a chance to win a hundred. Plus fifty boxes of chocolates. The cruel part—watching two guys hitting each other, maybe hurting each other, while they're safe in the bleachers. That's why it works, Carter, because we're all bastards."

Carter disguised his disgust. Archie repelled him in many ways but most of all by the way he made everybody feel dirty, contaminated, polluted. As if there was no goodness at all in the world. And yet Carter had to admit that he was looking forward to the fight, that he himself had bought not one but two tickets. Did that make him like everybody else— greedy and cruel, as Archie said? The question surprised him. Hell, he'd always thought of himself as one of the good guys. He had often used his position as president of The Vigils to keep control of Archie, to prevent him from going overboard on assignments. But did that make him one of the good guys? The question bothered Carter. That's what he hated about Archie. He made you feel guilty all the time. Christ, the world couldn't be as bad as Archie said it was. But hearing the shouts of the kids in the bleachers, impatient for the fight to get underway, Carter wondered.

Archie watched Carter drift away, looking troubled and perplexed. Great. Burning with jealousy. And who wouldn't be jealous of someone like Archie who always came out on top?

Cochran reported. "All sold out, Archie."

Archie nodded, assuming the role of the silent hero.

The moment was here.

Archie lifted his head toward the bleachers and it seemed to be some kind of signal. A ripple went through the crowd, a quickening of tempo, a sweep of suspense. All eyes were directed to the platform where Renault and Janza stood at diagonal corners.

In front of the platform stood a pyramid of chocolates—the last fifty boxes. The stadium lights burned bright.

Carter, gavel in hand, walked to the center of the platform. There was nothing to bang the gavel on so he simply raised it in the air.

The audience responded with applause, impatient shoutings, catcalls. "Let's go," someone yelled.

Carter gestured for silence.

But the silence had already fallen.

Archie, walking toward the platform for a close view of the proceedings, sucked in his breath, as if he were sipping this sweetest of all events. But he exhaled in surprise and stopped in his tracks as he saw Obie walk on the platform carrying the black box in his hands.

Obie smiled maliciously when he caught Archie standing there in surprise, his mouth wide open in astonishment. No one ever surprised the great Archie that way, and Obie's moment of triumph was a thing of beauty. He nodded toward Carter who was on his way to escort Archie to the platform.

Carter had been doubtful about using the black box, pointing out that this was not a Vigils meeting. How can we make Archie try for the marbles?

Obie had the answer, the kind of answer Archie himself would have given. "Because there are four hundred kids out there yelling for blood. And they don't care whose blood it is anymore. Everybody in the school knows about the black box—how can Archie back down?"

Carter pointed out that there was no guarantee that Archie would pull out the black marble. The black would mean he'd have to take on the position of one of the fighters. But there were five white marbles and only one black marble in the box. Archie's luck had held up throughout his career as the assigner—he had never drawn the black one.

"The law of averages," Obie had said to Carter. "He's going to have to draw two marbles—one for Renault, the other for Janza."

Carter had gazed steadily at Obie. "We couldn't
. . . ?" His voice curled into a question mark.

"We can't fix it, no way. Where could I find six
black marbles, for crying out loud? Anyway, Archie is
too smart—we could never con him. But we can
throw one hell of a scare into him. And who knows?
Maybe his luck has run out."

Thus, the agreement. Obie would emerge with the
black box at the moment before the drawings and the
fight began. And that's exactly what he was doing
now, crossing to the center of the platform as Carter
went down to meet Archie.

"You guys are really something else, aren't you?"
Archie said, pulling away from Carter's grip. "I can
walk up there alone, Carter. And I'll walk back again,
too."

Archie's fury was a cold hard ball in his chest but
he played it cool. As usual. He had a feeling nothing
could go wrong. I am Archie.

The sight of the black box stunned the gathering
into a silence more deep than before. Only members
of The Vigils and their victims had seen it. In the
garish stadium light, the box was revealed as worn
and threadbare, a small wooden container that might
have been a discarded jewelry box. And yet it was a
legend in the school. For potential victims, it was
possible deliverance, protection, a weapon to be used
against the might of The Vigils. Others doubted its
existence: Archie Costello would never allow that sort
of thing. But here was the black box now. Out in the
open. In front of the whole frigging school. And
Archie Costello looking at it, reaching out his hand to
draw the marble.

The ceremony took only a minute or so because
Archie insisted on getting it over quickly before
anyone knew what was going on. The less drama, the

better. Don't let Obie and Carter build it up. Thus, before any protest could be made, Archie had shot his hand out and pulled a marble from the box. White. Obie's jaw dropped in surprise. Things were moving too fast. He'd wanted Archie to squirm; he'd wanted the audience to realize what was going on here. He'd wanted to prolong the ceremony, get as much of the drama and suspense out of the situation as possible.

Archie's hand shot out again and it was too late for Obie to prevent the action. He drew in his breath.

The marble was hidden in Archie's closed fist. He held the fist out, toward the audience. Archie held his back stiff. The marble had to be white. He hadn't come this far to be denied at the last moment. He let a smile play over his lips as he faced the audience, gambling everything in his show of confidence.

He opened his palm and held up the marble for all to see.

White.

Chapter 37

The Goober arrived at the last moment and made his way through the turmoil to the top of the bleachers. He'd been reluctant to come. He had washed his hands of the school and its cruelties and hadn't wanted to witness Jerry's daily humiliations. The school also reminded him of his own betrayals and defections. For three days, he'd been home in bed. Sick. He wasn't at all sure whether he'd really been sick or whether his conscience had revolted, infecting his body, leaving him weak and nauseous. At any rate, the bed had become his private world, a small safe place without people, without The Vigils, without Brother Leon, a world with no chocolates to sell, no rooms to destroy, no people to destroy. But one of the guys called up and told him about the fight between Jerry and Janza. And how the raffle tickets would control the fight. The Goober had moaned in protest. The bed had become unbearable. He had tossed and turned all day, prowling the bed like an animal seeking sleep, oblivion. He didn't want to go to the fight—Jerry couldn't possibly win. But he couldn't stay in bed, either. Finally, desperate, he had gotten out of bed, and dressed hurriedly, ignoring the protests of his parents. He had taken the bus across town and walked half a mile to the stadium. Now, he huddled in the seat, looking down at the platform, listening to Carter explaining the rules of the crazy fight. Terrible.

"... and the kid whose written blow is the one that

ends the fight, either by knockout or surrender, receives the prize . . ."

But the crowd was impatient for the action to begin. Goober looked around. These fellows in the stands were known to him, they were classmates, but suddenly they'd become strangers. They stared feverishly down at the platform. Some of them were yelling. "Kill 'em, kill 'em . . ." The Goober shivered in the night.

Carter advanced to the center of the platform where Obie held a cardboard carton. Carter reached in and pulled out a piece of paper. "John Tussier," he called. "He's written down Renault's name." Murmurs of disappointment, a few scattered boos. "He wants Renault to hit Janza with a right to the jaw."

Silence fell. The moment of truth. Renault and Janza faced each other, an arm's reach away. They had been standing in the traditional pose of fighters, gloves raised, ready for battle but a pathetic parody of professional fighters. Now, Janza followed the rules. He lowered his arms, prepared to take Jerry's blow without resistance.

Jerry hunched his shoulders, cocked his fist. He had been waiting for this moment, ever since Archie's voice had taunted him on the telephone. But he hesitated now. How could he hit anyone, even an animal like Janza, in cold blood? I'm not a fighter, he protested silently. Then think of how Janza let those kids beat you up.

The crowd was restless. "Action, action," someone called. And the cry was taken up by others.

"What's the matter, fairy?" Janza taunted. "Afraid you might hurt your little hand hitting great big Emile?"

Jerry sent his fist sailing toward Janza's jaw, but he had swung too quickly, without sufficient aim. The blow almost missed its target, finally brushing Janza's jaw ineffectually. Janza grinned.

Boos filled the air. "Fix," someone called.

Carter motioned to Obie to bring the box out quickly. He sensed the impatience of the crowd. They had paid their money and they wanted action. He hoped Janza's name would be on this slip. And it was. A kid named Marty Heller had ordered Janza to hit Renault with a right uppercut to the jaw. Carter sang out the command.

Jerry planted himself, like a tree.

Janza got ready, insulted by the cries of *fix*. Just because Renault was chicken. I'm not chicken, I'll show them. He had to prove that this was a genuine contest. If Renault wouldn't fight, then at least Emile Janza would.

He struck Jerry with all the force he could summon, the impact of the blow coming from his feet, up through his legs and thighs, the trunk of his body, the power pulsing through his body like some elemental force until it erupted through his arm, exploding into his fist.

Jerry had girded himself for the blow but it took him by surprise with its savagery and viciousness. The entire planet was jarred for a moment, the stadium swaying, the lights dancing. The pain in his neck was excruciating—his head had snapped back from the impact of Janza's fist. Sent reeling backward, he fought to stay on his feet and he somehow managed not to fall. His jaw was on fire, he tasted acid. Blood, maybe. But he pressed his lips together. He shook his head, quick vision-clearing shakings and established himself in the world once more.

Before he could gather himself together again, Carter's voice cried out "*Janza, right to the stomach*" and Janza struck without warning, a short sharp blow that missed Jerry's stomach but caught him in the chest. His breath went away, like it did in football, and then came back again. But the blow had lacked the power of the uppercut. He crouched again, fists erect, waiting for the next instructions. Dimly, he heard the crowd both cheering and booing but he concentrated on Janza who stood before him, that idiot smile on his face.

The next raffle ticket gave Jerry his chance to strike back at Janza. A kid Jerry had never heard of— someone named Arthur Robilard—called for a right cross. Whatever that was. Jerry had only a vague idea but he wanted to hit Janza now, to repay him for that first vicious blow. He cocked his right arm. He tasted bile in his mouth. He let his arm go. The glove struck Janza full face and Janza staggered back. The result surprised Jerry. He had never struck anyone like that before, in fury, premeditated, and he'd enjoyed catapulting all his power toward the target, the release of all his frustrations, hitting back at last, lashing out, getting revenge finally, revenge not only against Janza but all that he represented.

Janza's eyes leaped with surprise at the strength behind Jerry's blow. His immediate reaction was to counterpunch but he held himself in control.

Carter's voice. "Janza. Left uppercut."

Again, the quick jolting neck-snapping pain as Janza, without pause or preparation, struck out. Jerry back-pedaled weakly. Why should his knees give way when the blow struck his jaw?

The guys were shouting from the bleachers for more action now. The noise chilled Jerry. "Action, action," came the shouts from the audience.

That was when Carter made the mistake. He took the slip of paper Obie handed him and read the instructions without pausing. "Janza, low blow to the groin." As soon as the words were out of his mouth, Carter realized his error. They hadn't warned the crowd about illegal punches—and there was always a wise guy out there ready to pull a fast one.

At the words, Janza aimed for Jerry's pelvic area. Jerry saw the fist coming. He raised his fists and looked toward Carter, sensing that something was wrong. Janza's fist sank into his lower stomach but Jerry had deflected part of the force of the blow.

The crowd didn't understand what had happened. Most of them hadn't heard the illegal instruction. They only saw that Jerry had tried to defend himself, and that was against the rules. "Kill 'im, Janza," a voice cried from the crowd.

Janza, too, was puzzled, but only for a moment. Hell, he'd followed instructions and here was Renault, the chicken, breaking the rules. The hell with the rules, then. Janza let his fists fly in a flurry of violence, hitting Renault almost at will, on the head, the cheeks, once in the stomach. Carter withdrew to the far side of the platform. Obie had fled the scene, sensing disaster. Where the hell was Archie? Carter couldn't see him.

Jerry did his best to build defenses against Janza's fists but it was impossible. Janza was too strong and too fast, all instinct, sensing a kill. Finally, Jerry covered his head and face with the gloves, letting the blows rain on him, but waiting, waiting. The crowd was in a turmoil now, shouting, jeering, urging Janza on.

One more shot at Janza, that's what Jerry wanted. Crouching, absorbing the attack, Jerry waited. There was something wrong with his jaw, the pain was intense, but he didn't care if he could hit Janza again, renew that earlier beautiful punch. He was being hit everywhere now and the crowd noises leaped to life as if someone had turned up the volume on a monstrous stereo.

Emile was getting tired. The kid wouldn't go down. He drew back his arm, pausing a moment, seeking true aim, wanting to come up with the final devastating blow. And that was when Jerry saw his opening. Through the pain and his nausea, he saw Janza's chest and stomach unprotected. He swung— and it was beautiful again. The full force of all his strength and determination and revenge caught Janza unguarded, off balance. Janza staggered backward, surprise and pain rampant on his face.

Triumphantly, he watched Janza floundering on weak, wobbly knees. Jerry turned toward the crowd, seeking—what? Applause? They were booing. Booing him. Shaking his head, trying to reassemble himself, squinting, he saw Archie in the crowd, a grinning, exultant Archie. A new sickness invaded Jerry, the sickness of knowing what he had become, another animal, another beast, another violent person in a violent world, inflicting damage, not disturbing the universe but damaging it. He had allowed Archie to do this to him.

And that crowd out there he had wanted to impress? To prove to himself before? Hell, they wanted him to lose, they wanted him killed, for Christ's sake.

Janza's fist caught him at the temple, sending Jerry reeling. His stomach caved in as Janza's fist sank into the flesh. He clutched at his stomach protectively and his face absorbed two stunning blows—his left eye felt smashed, the pupil crushed. His body sang with pain.

Horrified, The Goober counted the punches Janza was throwing at his helpless opponent. Fifteen, sixteen. He leaped to his feet. Stop it, stop it. But nobody heard. His voice was lost in the thunder of screaming voices, voices calling for the kill . . . *kill him, kill him.* Goober watched helplessly as Jerry finally sank to the stage, bloody, opened mouth, sucking for air, eyes unfocused, flesh swollen. His body was poised for a moment like some wounded animal and then he collapsed like a hunk of meat cut loose from a butcher's hook.

And the lights went out.

Obie would never forget that face.

A moment before the lights went out, he turned away from the platform, disgusted with the scene, the kid Renault being pummeled by Janza. The sight of blood always sickened him, anyway.

Looking away from the bleachers, he glanced up at a small hill that looked down at the field. The hill was actually huge rock imbedded in the landscape, partially covered with moss and also with scrawled obscenities that had to be scrubbed off almost daily.

A movement caught Obie's eye. That's when he saw the face of Brother Leon. Leon stood at the top of the hill, a black coat draped around his shoulders. In the reflection of the stadium lights, his face was like a gleaming coin. The bastard, Obie thought. He's been there all the time, I'll bet, watching it all.

The face vanished as the darkness fell.

The darkness was sudden and deep.

Like a giant ink blot poured over the bleachers, the platform, the entire field.

Like the world suddenly wiped out, devastated.

Goddam it, Archie thought, as he stumbled away from the bleachers toward the small utility building where the electrical controls were located.

He tripped, fell down, and groped to his feet.

Someone brushed past him. The noise from the

bleachers was awesome, kids screaming and shouting, guys tumbling from the seats. Small flames tore at the darkness as matches and cigarette lighters were lit.

Stupid, Archie thought, they're all stupid. He was the only one here with the presence of mind to check the cause of the power failure at the control building.

Tripping over a fallen body, Archie swiveled his way to the building, arms extended in front of him. As he reached the door, the lights went on again, blinding in their intensity. Dazed, blinking, he flung the door open and encountered Brother Jacques whose hand was on the switch.

"Welcome, Archie. I imagine you are the villain here, aren't you?" His voice was cool but his contempt was unmistakable.

Chapter 38

"Jerry."

Wet darkness. Funny, darkness shouldn't be wet. But it was. Like blood.

"Jerry."

But blood wasn't black. It was red. And he was surrounded by black.

"Come on, Jerry."

Come on where? He liked it here, in the darkness, moist and warm and wet.

"Hey, Jerry."

Voices outside the window calling. Shut the window, shut it. Shut the voices out.

"Jerry . . ."

Something sad in the voice now. More than sad—scared. Something scared in the voice.

Suddenly the pain verified his existence, brought him into focus. Here and now. Jesus, the pain.

"Take it easy, Jerry, take it easy," The Goober was saying, cradling Jerry in his arms. The platform was brilliantly lit again, like an operating table, but the stadium was almost empty, a few curious stragglers still hanging around. Bitterly, Goober had watched the guys leaving, chased away by Brother Jacques and a couple of other faculty members. The guys had vacated the place as if leaving the scene of a crime, strangely subdued. Goober had struggled toward the ring in the darkness and had finally reached Jerry as the lights went on. "We better get a doctor," he had yelled at the kid called Obie, Archie's stooge.

Obie had nodded, his face pale and ghostlike in the floodlights.

"Take it easy," Goober said now, drawing Jerry closer. Jerry felt broken. "Everything will be all right . . ."

Jerry raised himself toward the voice, needing to answer it. He had to answer. But he kept his eyes shut, as if he could keep a lid on the pain that way. But it was more than pain that caused an urgency in him. The pain had become the nature of his existence but this other thing weighed on him, a terrible burden. What other thing? The knowledge, the knowledge: what he had discovered. Funny, how his mind was clear suddenly, apart from his body, floating above his body, floating above the pain.

"It'll be all right, Jerry."

No it won't. He recognized Goober's voice and it was important to share the discovery with Goober. He had to tell Goober to play ball, to play football, to run, to make the team, to sell the chocolates, to sell whatever they wanted you to sell, to do whatever they wanted you to do. He tried to voice the words but there was something wrong with his mouth, his teeth, his face. But he went ahead anyway, telling Goober what he needed to know. They tell you to do your thing but they don't mean it. They don't want you to do your thing, not unless it happens to be their thing, too. It's a laugh, Goober, a fake. Don't disturb the universe, Goober, no matter what the posters say.

His eyes fluttered open and he saw Goober's face all askew, like on a broken movie film. But he was able to see the concern, the worry on his face.

Take it easy, Goober, it doesn't even hurt anymore. See? I'm floating, floating above the pain. Just remember what I told you. It's important. Otherwise, they murder you.

"Why did you do it to him, Archie?"

"I don't know what you're talking about."

Archie turned away from Brother Jacques and watched the ambulance making its careful progress out of the athletic field, the rotating blue light casting emergency flashings all over the place. The doctor said that Renault may have sustained a fracture of the jaw and there may be internal injuries. X-rays would tell. What the hell, Archie thought, those were the risks of the boxing ring.

Jacques swung Archie around. "Look at me when I talk to you," he said. "If someone hadn't come to the Residence and told me what was going on here, who knows how far it might have gone? What happened to Renault was bad enough, but there was violence in the air. You could have had a riot on your hands, the way those kids were stirred up."

Archie didn't bother to answer. Brother Jacques probably considered himself a hero for putting out the lights and stopping the fight. As far as Archie was concerned, Jacques had merely spoiled the evening. And Jacques had arrived too late anyway. Renault had already been beaten. Too fast, much too fast. Leave it to that stupid Carter to screw things up. Low blow, for crying out loud.

"What have you got to say for yourself, Costello?" Brother Jacques persisted.

Archie sighed. Bored, really. "Look, Brother, the school wanted the chocolates sold. And we got them sold. This was the payoff, that's all. A fight. With rules. Fair and square."

Leon was suddenly there with them, one arm clapped around Jacques' shoulder.

"I see you have everything under control, Brother Jacques," he said, heartily.

Jacques turned a cold face toward his fellow

teacher. "I think we barely averted a disaster," he said. There was rebuke in his voice but a gentle, guarded rebuke, not the hostility he had revealed to Archie. And Archie realized that Leon was still in command, still in the position of power.

"Renault will get the best of care, I assure you," Leon said. "Boys will be boys, Jacques. They have high spirits. Oh, once in a while they get carried away but it's good to see all that energy and zeal and enthusiasm." He turned to Archie and spoke more severely but not really angry. "You really didn't use your best judgment tonight, Archie. But I realize you did it for the school. For Trinity."

Brother Jacques stalked away. Archie and Leon watched him go. Archie smiled inside. But he masked his feelings. Leon was on his side. Beautiful. Leon and The Vigils and Archie. What a great year it was going to be.

The ambulance's siren began to howl in the night.

Chapter 39

"Someday, Archie," Obie said, a warning in his voice, "someday . . ."

"Cut it out, Obie. Enough preaching tonight. Brother Jacques already delivered a sermon to me." Archie chuckled. "But Leon came to the rescue. Good man, that Leon."

They were sitting in the bleachers, watching some of the guys cleaning up the place. This was where they had first seen Renault that afternoon Archie had selected him for the assignment. The night had grown cold and Obie shivered slightly. He looked at the goal posts. They reminded him of something. He couldn't remember.

"Leon is a bastard," Obie said. "I saw him on the hill over there—watching the fight, enjoying the whole thing."

"I know," Archie said. "I tipped him off. An anonymous phone call. I figured he would enjoy himself. And I also figured that if he was here and part of the proceedings, he'd also be protection for us if anything went wrong."

"Someday, Archie, you'll get yours," Obie said but the words were automatic. Archie was always one step ahead.

"Look, Obie, I'm going to forget what you did tonight—you and Carter and the black box. What the hell, it was a dramatic moment. And I understand how you felt. My understanding of you and guys like Carter is a marvel to behold." He had lapsed into his phony way of speaking when he wanted to be fancy or sarcastic.

"Maybe the black box will work the next time, Archie," Obie said. "Or maybe another kid like Renault will come along."

Archie didn't bother to answer. Wishful thinking wasn't worth answering. He sniffed the air and yawned. "Hey, Obie, what happened to the chocolates?"

"The guys raided the chocolates in the confusion. As far as the money's concerned, Brian Cochran has it. We'll have some kind of drawing next week at assembly."

Archie barely listened. He wasn't interested. He was hungry. "You sure all the chocolates are gone, Obie?"

"I'm sure, Archie."

"You got a Hershey or anything?"

"No."

The lights went off again. Archie and Obie sat there awhile not saying anything and then made their way out of the place in the darkness.

Related Readings

CONTENTS

I took my Power in my Hand—

by Emily Dickinson

*Another writer, 19th-century poet Emily
Dickinson, considers what can happen
when an individual goes against the larger
world. The speaker in her poem compares
himself or herself to the Biblical David,
who fought the giant warrior Goliath
(Goliah). The speaker's ending question
could also be asked about Jerry in*
The Chocolate War.

I took my Power in my Hand—
And went against the World—
'Twas not so much as David—had—
But I—was twice as bold—

5   I aimed my Pebble—but Myself
Was all the one that fell—
Was it Goliah—was too large—
Or was myself—too small?

Some Opposites of Good

by Leslie Norris

Leslie Norris draws on his childhood in Wales in the 1920s and 1930s for many of his stories and poems. This story is set in a strict boys' school where disorderly or unprepared students can expect physical punishment from their teachers and headmaster. Compare what little Mark learns in school to what Jerry learns.

When Mark opened the front door he could see Useless Lewis waiting for him at the corner of the street. Useless was poised in a tense crouch, his face tight and snarling. Without mercy he gunned down Mr. Sweet's black cat, pumping bullets into its rich fur as it sat sunning itself in the doorway of the shop; then, straightening, he sprayed the street with bullets, smiling grimly at the patterned dust he raised.

"Goodbye, Mark," called Mark's mother from her kitchen.

Useless sweetly holstered the clenched fists of his imagined six-shooters, caught invisible reins in the tips of his fingers, and cantered down the road, slapping his haunches with the flat of his hand, whinnying. Useless was being the world's greatest cowboy.

"Hi," he said to Mark.

On the way to school nothing escaped the vigilance of Useless' accurate fingers. He shot the tops from bottles of milk as they stood in doorways, he blasted passing cyclists as they sped innocently to work, he exploded the wheels of cars. At street corners he stood six feet tall, surveying the scene with his bleak, sardonic eye before calling Mark forward to walk in safety among the traps and ambushes laid in the shadows of the morning streets. Useless shot his way through them all. He was Mark's best friend, but he was an awful nuisance. Mark was glad when they got to school.

Although it was early, Jack Mathias would certainly be there before them. Jack Mathias lived a long way off, in a cottage on the mountain, and his mother was dead. When Mr. Mathias went to work, very early, Jack would have to leave too, because his father would lock the house. Jack would have to wait alone in the school yard until someone came along to talk to him. He had dirty teeth and his shirts were always crumpled and dirty because of his mother, but everybody liked him. He was fifteen years old, a big boy and a great footballer, the best in school. He was teaching Mark to play.

They played in the open shed that ran down one side of the yard, where the boys sheltered when it was raining. It was paved with granite slabs, a yard square, made smooth and polished by the running boots of generations of boys. Jack Mathias was waiting there, in the shade of the roof. Between his feet he had the little flat stone they used instead of a ball and he was flicking it gently this way and that, absorbed in the performance of his faultless skill.

Useless was already stalking up the yard, stiff-legged and menacing, ready to shoot it out with any black evil, the thunder of his avenging guns held silent under his thumbs.

"Keck! Keck!" he said, bringing down two passing crows.

Mark ran into the shed.

"Right," said Jack Mathias, "you get five goals start, OK?"

They ran until the shed was so full of boys they could no longer play without interruption, and then Jack Mathias showed Mark how to swerve and how to push the ball around one side of an opponent and run around the other.

"You'll have to learn to use your left foot," said Jack Mathias. "Watch this."

He collected the stone with a cool sweep of his leg and, in the same movement, pushed it in front of him. But even as he jumped into his first stride, his right knee raised, the whole world stopped. Jack Mathias hung, arrested in midflight, long arms aloft. The little stone went bobbling on, scuttling over the flagstones, making a tiny hollow noise, the only moving thing in the school yard. Everywhere groups of boys held their frozen attitudes, older boys like careless and lounging statues, small boys balancing precariously at the edges of energy. The first whistle had gone, and nobody must move. Mark, without the stir of a visible muscle, got ready for the second whistle. When it came, he shot into action, racing for the class lines in front of the school building. But he was a long way off and had to find a place near the end of the queue. Useless was four or five boys in front of him, and Mark waved to him. But Useless didn't see him. Useless had gone to live inside his head, he was galloping the wide and sunlit prairies of his imagination.

The teacher on duty was Witty Thomas, small, plump and beautifully dressed. This morning he wore a suit of silver-gray and his shirt was a rich cream color. His tie was red with little silver flowers woven in it, and the fresh rose in his buttonhole was as yellow as sunshine. He bounced about in front of the files of boys, his face pink, sending his thin voice shouting into the air, waving his arms at the sauntering impertinence of the older boys as they came slowly into a reluctant line.

"Come, come on!" screamed Mr. Thomas. "Do you think you've got all day?"

The big boys idled along, some smiling openly at histrionic Mr. Thomas, some, their heads turned away, ignoring him.

Witty, in an impotent fury, danced toward them on his little glittering shoes, and, as he came near, Useless, concentrating, steadying his aim with the coldest deliberation, shot away, one after the other, the pearl buttons on Mr. Thomas' vest. He was narrowing his eyes to focus on the last button when Mr. Thomas saw him.

"What's this?" cried Witty Thomas, suddenly and terrifyingly jovial. "And what is this? Would you like to shoot me, Lewis?"

He grabbed Useless by the collar and pulled him out, shaking him and jerking him. Mark could see the nailed soles of Useless' boots as his legs swung in the air.

A small, delighted cheer came from the boys, but Mr. Thomas ignored it. He just smiled his frightening smile and began to cuff Useless' head.

"So you'd like to shoot me, eh, Lewis?" Witty Thomas said. "But you wouldn't dare, would you, would you, would you!"

He punctuated his speech with quick slaps, but Useless cleverly burrowed close to him, burying his head against Mr. Thomas' round little stomach so that the man couldn't swing at him.

"Leave him alone," shouted Jack Mathias in his laughing, man's voice. "Pick someone your own size! Go it little 'un!"

Everybody knew that Mr. Thomas was afraid to touch Jack Mathias, because Jack's father was so big and rough.

Useless came back to his place and he was smiling all over. He wasn't frightened, Mark could see that.

"Fifty years old," said Damion Davies, who was tall and thin and lazy. "Fifty years old and still heavyweight champion. Just fancy!"

"Shut it, Davies," said Mr. Thomas, panting, "or you'll get the same."

"Such a temper, too," said Damion in his languid voice, and he rolled his eyes in mock admiration.

"Lead on!" cried Mr. Thomas, pointing, as if he were leading an expedition into wildest Tibet. "Lead on, the first row!"

Useless and Mark bent their knees and slid into the cold, stiff hinged desk they shared, being careful of the splinters, sharp as frost, that would run into their thighs. They took out their books and placed them neatly, ready for work. Mark looked at his friend. The marks of Mr. Thomas' grabbing fingers were plain on the back of Useless' neck and his right ear was blazing red. You could almost warm your hands against it.

"Does it hurt?" Mark whispered.

"Of course not," said Useless, "Witty couldn't hurt a fly."

Useless couldn't read. Each morning Mark would have to help him, listening to him mutter aloud the separate, clumsy words as he stumbled from sentence to sentence. Mark worked hard with Useless. He had stood for hours outside shops, making Useless read the price cards and the advertisements for chocolates, but it was no use. It was as if words had no meaning for Useless. He could not see that they added to each other as you said them, that the sum of the words was interesting and surprising. He listened to Useless drop the flat sounds one by one out of his mouth.

"Don't forget," said Useless between sentences. "It's Friday, pass it on."

Most Friday mornings Mr. Treharne, the headmaster, came in to test the boys in spelling, in mental arithmetic and in the plurals and opposites of words. Mark enjoyed this. He would sit upright in his desk, his arms folded in front of him, hoping Mr. Treharne would ask him some spectacularly difficult question. When this happened Mark's mind would become as clear as glass and he would see the answer right in the center of his thinking. But very often Mr. Treharne didn't ask him anything at all, preferring to spend his time being angry at those poor boys who couldn't answer anything. Useless was one of these.

It was strange about Useless. He was brave, he was loyal, he knew a lot of jokes. When he pretended, you could believe in the unseen world Useless would make around him. Mark just knew, just from watching Useless, that he had ridden a white horse to school that morning, you could see it. Although your real eyes would still see only a boy with short hair and freckles on his neck. Useless knew about real horses, too. His father had a pony and cart and one Sunday in the summer the boys had gone to a field near the river and caught the pony. Useless had held an apple in his hand and the pony had eaten it, very gently, with his crude brown teeth. Then Useless had leapt cleverly on the animal's back, wrapping the coarse hair of its mane in his fists. He'd hung on for a long while as the pony galloped clumsily around the field. A horse was unexpectedly heavy. Mark could remember the surprising weight of its hooves when they pounded the earth like an immense drum. In the end Useless had fallen off and lay on his back, puffing and laughing. He hoped Useless would be able to answer some of Mr. Treharne's questions. He looked over at Useless and his ear was pretty nearly the normal color.

Mr. Pascoe, their own teacher, put his hand gently on Mark's shoulder, reminding him to get on with his work. The boy bent his head over his book and began to write. Mr. Pascoe was young and kind and this was his very first job. All the boys liked him. As he wrote, Mark still thought of Useless, fallen and laughing in the grass by the river, remembering too the dark green of the clover patches, and their pink flowers. Mark began to write a story of two friends who had gone to a summer field and found there a horse so gentle, its breath so fragrant of sweet clover, so amenable and intelligent an animal that it was more companion than beast. It was thin, and seemed to have been cruelly treated, but there was about it a recognizable air of breeding, of a royal pride. For weeks, in the story, the two boys had coveted the horse, exulting in its increasing strength and beauty. Mark began to describe the glowing perfection of his coat, its docile manner, its unassuming pride. There was no doubt, Mark felt, that here he was making a prince among horses, a true Arabian. He was about to send all three of his heroes on some epic journey when the headmaster walked in.

Mark slowly put away his story. He would have liked to have returned his lovely pony to its true owner, an eagle-profiled sheikh who lived in a camp high in the Atlas Mountains. After years of adventure, the boys would have handed over the superb horse. They would have been rewarded with jewels, made members of this most savage of Bedouin tribes. A great feast would have been made in their honor, with kebabs and raw sheep's eyes. They would have flown home famous and wealthy.

"Hurry up, boy," said Mr. Treharne, tapping Mark's desk with his cane.

Mr. Treharne was not big, but he walked with compensating dignity and importance. He carried with him his own silence, hard and painful, and it was this sensation that filled the room now, as cold water might fill a bowl. Mr. Treharne put his cane under his arm and drew back his lips in a grimace, revealing white teeth regular and artificial as a doll's.

Mr. Pascoe stood nervously near his high desk.

"Sit down, Pascoe," said Mr. Treharne. "Sit down, man. Where's your chalk?"

He took some chalk from the table and stood before the boys. The air in the room was so still that Mark thought he could have plucked it like a guitar string. Then the testing began.

It was not too bad. First they did some multiplication tables and then questions about buying and selling things, buns, postage stamps, gallons of milk. Mr. Treharne spoke very slowly and clearly, making sure every boy had heard; and then he'd pounce, his rigid cane pointed at arm's length, on some unready boy. He knew exactly which poor boys would find the questions impossible to answer. But most of them were prepared and alert, answering Mr. Treharne confidently. It was going to be a happy morning. Even Mr. Treharne was nearly smiling.

He turned about slowly, looking meditatively from one boy's face to another, but Mark wasn't fooled. He knew better than to relax.

"Galaxy," Mr. Treharne snapped, his stick under Mark's nose. "You boy, spell galaxy."

That was an easy one.

"You're a sharp lad," said Mr. Treharne, "a bright lad."

He leaned away as if to ask some other boy a word, and then whipped back.

"Idiosyncracy," he said.

Flawlessly and successively Mark spelled idiosyncracy, brontosaurus, yacht, zephyr, seraph, commission.

Mark was elated. It was like playing some vitally skillful and dangerous game, in which Mr. Treharne was attacking him with something as sharp and violent as a sword, and only by the most agile and determined techniques could Mark beat him away. When the headmaster asked him no more words Mark knew he had won. He felt hard and shining, as if every bit of him was clean and smooth, working with a silent perfection. He imagined all the world's words waiting for him to order them into formal and meticulous patterns. He sat upright on his bench, his back achingly straight, triumphant. It was a little time before he could listen to what was happening in the room.

Mr. Treharne was no longer pleased. David Sheppard and Ronnie Howells were standing up, their hands behind their backs, unable to give the opposite of sour, and Mr. Treharne was clicking his tongue in irritation. Two little red spots appeared on his cheekbones. Mark looked about; nobody appeared to know. He put up his hand.

"Put down your hand, Watkins," snarled Mr. Treharne, not looking at him. "You've had your moment of splendor. Are you idiot enough to think that you alone know the opposite of sour?"

Mark pulled his hand down. Somebody tittered.

"The next boy to laugh," said Mr. Treharne, "will

find I have a painful cure for that condition. It is no matter for amusement to find we have two ignorant and lazy boys in a class."

His face was sullen, the corners of his mouth drawn sternly down.

"The opposite of sour is sweet," he said. "Sweet. Do you hear me, Howells, Sheppard? Sit down. I have no patience with you."

He watched the two boys sit. There was not a sound in the room, not even a breath. Little Frankie Rossi, the smallest boy in the class, stared terrified in front of him. Then he began, very slightly, to tremble.

Cautiously the boys waited, careful to do nothing that would disturb the man's dry temper, inflammable as straw.

"There will be others," said Mr. Treharne, "other boys, lazy fellows all of them, who will not be able to answer the simplest of questions!"

The boys shivered as he looked at them.

"Rossi, for example," shouted Mr. Treharne.

It was not fair to pick on Frankie Rossi. Although he was small, he was always cheerful and smiling. He and Useless were the worst readers in the class.

"Rossi," said Mr. Treharne, "give us the benefit of your erudition. Give us the opposites of long, dry, little, thin, good."

He spat out each word, his face red and angry, cracking the face of the table with his cane, each stroke leaving a clean brown mark in the film of chalk dust on the surface.

Frankie Rossi began to cry, softly and quietly. Mr. Pascoe was standing behind the headmaster, his face pale, perfectly still except for his hands. His fingers were lifting and falling against the cloth of his jacket. There was no other movement.

Then Mr. Treharne was striding between the desks,

asking boy after boy for opposites to those simple words. It was as if a great storm, an unimaginable violence, had entered the familiar room and ripped away its safety. Mr. Treharne moved and spoke with such fury that nobody had time to answer him.

At last he stopped, so close to Mark that the boy could feel his nearness. Mr. Treharne was looking at Useless.

"And now we come to Lewis," said Mr. Treharne, almost whispering.

Useless stood in his desk, his legs bent where the bench pressed against the back of his knees. The whole desk was shaking slightly, as if it was alive.

"Lewis," said Mr. Treharne, "I want you to tell me the opposite of good. Tell us all, Lewis, we shall await your answer."

Mark let out his breath in relief. He had been praying as intensely as he knew how, willing Mr. Treharne to ask Useless something easy. Now everything would be all right.

But Useless did not answer.

"Think hard, Lewis," said Mr. Treharne. "Think hard. It will be the cane if you do not give me the correct answer."

Mark could see Useless' legs quivering, he could almost smell his fear. In an agony, Mark urged his friend to speak, sending the silent words across to him.

Useless lifted his head.

"Rotten, sir," he blurted.

The brilliance and unexpectedness of Useless' word were like the sunshine, lighting up Mark's mind. He turned in astonishment to his friend, almost clapping aloud.

"Keep still, Watkins," Mr. Treharne said to him.

He whipped his cane through the air, making a pliant and cruel whistling.

"Come out, Lewis," he said.

Mr. Treharne could not have heard Useless. Mark put up his hand to explain.

"Put down your hand," shouted Mr. Treharne, in a sudden explosion of renewed temper, "I shan't tell you again."

But Mark knew there was a mistake. He smiled up at Mr. Treharne.

"But sir," he said, "Useless' father, sir, he keeps a fruit shop, and he sells the good apples, sir, and he throws away the rotten . . ."

"Come out, Watkins," said Mr. Treharne.

Mark scrambled out of his desk and stood beside Useless.

"Hold out your hand," Mr. Treharne said to Useless.

Mark could not think that it was happening, that Mr. Treharne could have failed to understand the wonderful accuracy of Useless' word. He was confused and indignant.

"Sir," he said, "you mustn't cane him. Rotten is a good opposite!"

And suddenly Mr. Treharne was before him, grabbing Mark's wrist with terrifying ferocity, pulling the boy's arm out straight before him. He rapped Mark's knuckles sharply with the cane to open the hand. Then he raised the stick above his head and brought it cutting down on the small flesh in a full arc, across the base of the palm and the soft fingers. At first there was no pain at all, for a slight moment only, and then an agony so far beyond anything he had experienced before took away the boy's breath and left him gasping. He could not see anything and was only dimly aware that at his side Useless was being punished in his turn. Mr. Treharne bundled the shocked boys into their seats. Mark held his burning hand between his knees and put his head on the hard wood of the desk so that nobody could see his weeping face.

After Mr. Treharne had left the room, Mr. Pascoe came over to Mark, talking quietly to him, trying to help him. The bell rang for morning break and Mr. Pascoe let Mark stay in the room and Useless stayed with him.

"The pain'll go after a bit," Useless said.

But all through the morning, long after he was able to look objectively at his beaten hand and touch the swollen skin of his fingers, the boy would shake with occasional sobs. He mourned not so much for his vanishing pain, nor the indignity of his beating, but because his safe world had collapsed about him. He wept because he had been shown a world without hope and without justice, a world in which the very words were without meaning.

It's Fun Being in Power

by Maria Hinojosa

How much does Archie Costello have in common with a young gang leader from New York City? In 1990, National Public Radio reporter Maria Hinojosa (ē´ nō hō´ sä) interviewed 17-year-old Coki (not his real name), a founding member of the "crew" called FTS, or Flushing's Top Society. He tries to explain his cold outlook and destructive life in Crews: Gang Members Talk to Maria Hinojosa.

Coki says the only thing that's perfect in this world is a newborn baby. And he says the two people he admires most in this world are Dr. Martin Luther King and John Lennon because they both had impossible dreams. He worries about the environment and the ozone layer, and he wishes he could work with animals, like a zoologist. *Scarface* is Coki's all-time favorite movie. He knows almost all the lines.

Coki has also been hanging out since he was about eight years old. It's not that he ever really chose to do it, but in a lot of ways, the street was a safer and more secure place for him than his house.

Coki, who was born in Ecuador but raised in Queens, has a hard time believing in himself. When he was in the seventh grade he was in the advanced students' classes, but he says he flipped on school and his grades went downhill. He ended up in special education classes for slow learners.

coki: The world was built on greed. The world runs on major power. Money power, political power, social power. It's common sense. I've known that for years. The world runs on greed and political power runs on arms, so you know the one with the most money and the most guns is the winner. That's the same way it is on the streets. The meanest guy on the block with the biggest knife or the biggest gun and the biggest pocket wins. It's fun being in power, or trying to claim the power, or trying to prove something. I used to walk into this store and walk out with cameras in my hand. When I was fourteen. I did it 'cause I knew how to get away with it. I did it because it was easy. Anything you can get away with, why not do it? You just feel smarter than the law. Especially when at home your mom is kicking and smacking . . . you, and all that's going on inside of you is, I hate you! Then you can't go outside with a Kool-Aid smile and be nice to everybody. . . . No matter how much I'm getting smacked up by my mother or my father, it's not like you can just make a fist and go, boom! But you hit your kid, he'll go outside and hit someone else. How would you like to be eight years old and be thrown out of your house on a Christmas night? My parents got into a fight and my father took me with him to his sister's house; he grabbed me and took me with him. Three days later Christmas came, and he sent me back to my mother, and she opens the door and says, "Get outta here! What do you want?" On a Christmas night! . . . So I turn around and I leave and half a block later my aunt comes running after me and takes me back home. . . . There's no reason to care. You go on the street and before anybody can get close to hurt you, you gotta hurt them.

But I'm a compassionate guy. If I feel sorry for you I won't hit you. See, I think every man should have compassion, because if you don't have compassion then you're an animal. If you're an animal, then you have no control. If you have no control, you can be easily manipulated. Once you're manipulated then you're a simple soldier. A robot.

My thing was just to win. I mean, I hated everything, except winning. I hated people. But I'm a fair person and if I see that you don't deserve something bad then if I can do something about it I won't let it happen to you.

My whole life has been a whole big mess. Like trouble, fighting, screaming, yelling, every day . . . practically every day . . . I think I can honestly name only one person who cared. My teacher. And my ex-girlfriend, but I let her go.

mh: What about the crew?

coki: That was my team. That was what I cared for. That was like the family. That's who was looking out for me in the streets and that's who I was looking out for in the street. It was my other family. On the other hand my family didn't want me hanging around with all those "criminals." I got into a lot of trouble hanging out with these guys, but, hey, that's my team. I coulda done that or I coulda went to school, and I'd probably be in a good college right now, but, hey, I would have missed out on a lot. I loved my teenage life. I was like the king of my school. I had the girlies and I had the respect. What mostly made me mean and mad and angry was what happened when I was like seven or eight or nine years old. Bam, bam, bam! Getting blamed for things you didn't do. Getting hit with a broomstick, bam, bam! Boom! And you being afraid of your moms and having to hide under the bed 'cause your mother was gonna get you. I was always getting blamed 'cause I was the one in the middle, between the oldest and the youngest. . . .

mh: Were you ever scared?

coki: Can't say never. Never say never. But would I ever get scared? I don't think so. But then again, if you have no fear then there's a problem. If you have no fear it means you're not alert, you're not aware. But if you're scared, then all your senses are going. And then you catch everything. But you never let anybody know that you're scared or they think they can control you. It's good to be confident but not good to be cocky.

mh: A lot of what you're saying is how you operate in the real world, too. In a job interview you can never let them see that you're scared.

coki: That's how governments are run. Except that in the streets, it's a dictatorship, but in the United States it's a democracy. I know the whole scoop, though.

mh: What is the whole scoop?

coki: Come on! I mean, eight or nine people run like 88 percent of the country.
　　The crews are the same thing politically like what rules the world. The head of the crew will be the toughest guy, and then the president of the toughest crew, which is the United States, he's got the congress, and like a crew's congress is like his peers. And the

gang leader might like his neighborhood to be a certain way, and the president might like his country to be a certain way. So they all use the same forms to run things in the same ways, except in different levels of government it's much larger and it's got more power. So it's the power I look for. It's like a little boy's dream that he might go to war. When kids are born, you know, they're not born racist, you're not born dumb, you're not born bad. All these things are put into your head when you're a kid. Like boys should act like this, and boys play with soldiers and tanks and they shoot each other up. So that you grow up wanting the power because when you play with your toy soldiers, one side is going to win. And if you grow up thinking that one side won and they did it with guns, then you want that. So you think, I want to go into the military and get a gun. Maybe one day I'll go to war and win. But I guess I just didn't care enough about myself to make it happen. I realized I had a problem back when I was little and part of the problem was that I didn't care. It was like neglection. People don't realize, but the home environment does shape a kid. Like if you're in fear when you're at home . . . or else you're scared 'cause you think your parents are gonna separate or break up. It means a lot to a kid to have his parents stay together. But if you're in this constant fear you're gonna take the fear and turn it into rage and that's not good.

One day in the future, when I'm stable, I'll be happy. I know it. 'Cause no matter how much I get kicked in the face, I always get up. I can put things behind me. I have so many memories behind me now—so many bad memories, but I don't let them stop me. I don't want to be in the park when I'm like thirty years old, sipping on some juice. I ain't down with that.

Breaking Bones

by Philip Cioffari

*Boys learn to bully each other long before
they get to high school, as you may know.
This painful poem shows how tragic and
permanent the effects of childhood
bullying can be.*

Take his lunchbox.
Pass around the peanut butter sandwich,
   the apple, the chocolate cookies.
Pull the bread apart, grind each half into
   the cement.
Play stickball with the apple.

5   Scale his cookies, one by one, at passing cars.
Grab his book bag, tear out the pages
   for tonight's homework,
write dirty words in red crayon on all
   the covers.
Load his gloves with stones,
sink them in the black muck of a sewer.

10   Swipe his hat and piss in it;
if he fights back, everyone jump him at once.
Track him down after school, on Saturdays
   and Sundays.
Gang up on him at all the following places:
street corners, bus stops, movie theatres,
   bars, offices, parties, dreams.

15   Fix it so when you're not around,
   he'll do it for you.
Fix it so he spends lunch hours,
   a lifetime by himself.
Fix him good.

White Places

by Mary Flanagan

If The Vigils were a gang of grade-school girls instead of high-school boys, their bullying might take the form it does in this story.

Celeste was first cousin to Cissy and Killer. Peachey was Celeste's Best, meaning her best friend. They always said 'Bests' to keep their true relationship a secret, and to be able to talk about the secret without hurting anyone else's feelings. That was the important thing, Celeste said, that no one know and that no one get their feelings hurt. Of course Cissy and Killer knew, but that was all right because they were first cousins to Celeste and so practically first cousins to Peachey.

The four of them had a club. The name and nature of this club was changed every three or four weeks, depending on what Celeste was reading. Celeste talked like a book and was fond of titles. She liked being President, Secretary, Madam Chairman and Grand Duchess Genevra Samantha Roberta della Rocca of Upper Vernocopium, a place even more important than Oz. The others let her be. But everyone knew it was Cissy who ruled.

Killer was the youngest and the fattest. Her shoes were always wet and untied with her socks sliding down into the heels. She had cold sores and was only in fourth grade. Her name was not really Killer. It was Charlotte Mundy Fletcher Doyle (mixed marriage: Roman Catholic and Presbyterian). Like just about every awful thing, the nickname was an invention of Cissy's. It came from one of their earliest games in which she and Celeste, starlets sharing an apartment in Beverly Hills, were stalked by a dangerous maniac known simply as The Killer. Their pretend boyfriends, a producer and his brother, the world's most daring stunt man, came over and over again to their rescue. Over and over they carried off Killer, bound and gagged, to a lunatic asylum. That was how it began—a crude game by later standards, but the name stuck. Cissy's and Celeste's parents tried, without success, to stop the children calling her by it.

'Chaaaaarrrrrrrrrlotte,' Cissy would sneer across the dinner table, 'pass the potatoes, Chaaaaarrrrrrrrlotte.' Cissy wasn't afraid of anything. Eventually though, when she behaved like this, she would be sent off to bed where she would lie awake, waiting to pinch her sister's fingers with the nutcracker as soon as she fell asleep, which was usually within three minutes.

Mrs. Doyle insisted the others be nice to Killer, share with her. Once she even had cried when her youngest daughter came home wet, though uncomplaining, from the swamp. They had been on a Royal Expedition up the Nile, led by Robert Redford and Cissy in a sedan chair. Killer had been thrown to the crocodiles after attempting to kidnap the baby Moses. Later, Killer had listened with her ear to the door as her mother reprimanded Cissy.

'Cissy, why are you so mean to Killer—' She stopped impatiently. 'Oh for heaven's sake, you know I mean *Charlotte*.' It was too late. Mummy had said it and that made it true forever.

Killer was six then, and Cissy was eight. By now the Pretends were much more complicated, and included a wide range of malice and glamour. (Cissy was maddeningly inventive.) But they were still variants on a single theme, and always ended with the Finding Out, the unmasking, at which everyone ran shrieking from Killer. Why the others liked pretending to be weak and frightened and in danger when really they were so strong, stronger than she would ever be, Killer could not understand.

A tried and true Pretend, used when all else had ended in boredom, or hair-pulling, was The Crazy Doctor. Killer, in disguise, would come to the grown-ups' bedroom—it had to begin in there—to prescribe for one of the three, who were always orphaned sisters. Eventually, they would guess her wicked intentions and race, screaming and laughing, to the attic, down again, through the upstairs rooms and out on to the lawn, pursued by Killer who was well-versed in the terrifying snorts and snarls she was required to make. Once outside, she would be caught, rolled up in a blanket, tied and taken off to be burnt at the stake, then released and made to play her part all over again until parents put a stop to the game.

They spent school vacations at each other's houses. Easter at the Doyles' and Christmas at Celeste's. This time, Peachey would be with them. Peachey was too small for her age, but very energetic. She was called Peachey because she once had been taught by her father to respond, at the top of her chipmunk voice to all enquiries after her condition with the answer 'Peachey Keeno!'

Celeste's father and mother were very indulgent. Even when the girls kept them awake until four in the morning, they did not complain very much. Killer always fell asleep first. The others ate crackers in bed and pushed the crumbs on to her side. They made raids to the kitchen for peanut butter sandwiches at two a.m. They came back and covered Killer's face with toothpaste. By the beam of a flashlight, they held a club meeting and read comic books under the covers. Peachey wrapped all their apple cores in paper and put the bundle down the toilet. The next morning the plumbing was blocked, and Killer stood, serious-eyed (she had been banished by the girls until three), watching Auntie Lillian mop up the bathroom on her hands and knees. She was given a jelly doughnut and allowed to watch Tom and Jerry until called to come and be a werewolf.

There was a blizzard. Killer was frightened by the silence and by the way the snow climbed the window panes. When she pressed her face against them, she imagined that she had gone blind, but that her blindness was white instead of black. It seemed hard to breathe, and she wondered if everyone were going to be buried alive. She thought she might like to go home. It would be nice to be tucked in by her mother and to watch her baby brother kicking his feet like a small fat bug or dribbling breakfast down his pyjamas. But she was too scared to tell Auntie Lillian any of these things. Besides, she had to stay here and be a Body Snatcher.

Celeste said that they should make puppets and a theatre and put on a puppet show. They thought of nothing else for the three days the blizzard lasted. Cissy and Celeste wrote a play and made posters to advertise the event, while Peachey and Killer worked happily and messily with balloons, cardboard tubes and papier mâché. Aunt Lillian was very patient. She and Uncle Raymond, along with all of Celeste's and Peachey's dolls, were forced to attend three per-formances, and to applaud, exclaim and congratulate on each occasion.

They experimented with the left-over flour and water paste, and invented, by the addition of sugar, milk, vanilla, corn syrup and a dash of laundry starch, a drink which they called Plush and which they forced Killer to taste after the addition of each new ingredient. That evening Killer threw up her supper. Cissy said that she thought it was disgusting, and that Killer was not mature enough to have been allowed to come.

When the storm ended, they put up signs and tried to sell Plush from a snow fort which they built at the end of the driveway. The snow was very high there, nearly six feet, because the blizzard had been such a long one and the snowplough had had to come around so many times. No one bought the drink but Uncle Raymond who tasted it, tried to smile, and said he would finish the rest in the house, if that was all right with 'you girls.' They lost interest in Plush. It turned sour, stank and Auntie Lillian carefully asked permission to throw it out.

They decided to enlarge the snow fort. They built half a dozen each winter and knew everything about their construction. This was to be the biggest they had ever made. To celebrate its completion, Cissy said, they must make up a brand new Pretend. Celeste agreed. Then Peachey and Killer agreed. They worked even harder on the snow fort than they had on the puppet show, talking and planning every minute for the Important Celebration Pretend. They were very excited, Killer could tell. She saw how much it thrilled them to make believe. To her, inside, it seemed almost frightening, the way they were always at it, never, never getting tired of it. Why did they want to be something they weren't, to change everything into what it wasn't? Killer liked everything as it was—just plain with no Pretend, no titles, no talking like books, no ruling, no dressing up, no punishments, no Madam Chairman or Grand Duchesses or Cleopatras. But that was her secret. She knew that somehow it was wrong to like everything as it was, just plain. So she didn't dare tell them what she really liked.

What she liked was what they were doing now: sitting on top of their snow fort, watching people go by on the street—slipping and sliding, it was so funny—smelling the snow and sucking silently on the long icicles that hung from the maple trees and that tasted so sweet. Killer sat and sucked and felt happy to be with the others, happy about not having to do fractions, happy about the graham crackers and marshmallow they would be eating at four when Pretend was over.

Peachey, in a burst of Peachey energy, put snow down the back of her neck. Killer was soaked through anyway. They all were. But they hardly noticed, they were so warm with activity.

'Now this is the game,' Cissy announced, 'and you have to remember it. We've decided, so no changing the rules. Me and Celeste and Peachey are sisters and we're of noble birth. Our *real* mother dies and our father the Duke marries this woman Elvira, who pretends to be nice but who isn't—who's evil really. That's you Killer. You have to *seem* nice at first, remember that otherwise you'll spoil everything. Then we find out that Elvira has killed our *real* mother and is plotting to kill our father and steal our inheritance and make us homeless orphans. Then—this is Celeste's part, she invented it, she says I have to say so—a prince saves us! He catches Elvira making a cowardly escape. Then he marries Celeste and introduces me and Peachey to his two brothers who are Paul Newman and Steve McQueen. Elvira goes to prison. Do you hear that, Killer? Are you listening? You're going to be shut up in the snow fort—don't interrupt me, you *have* to be. Do you want to spoil the game for everyone else? That *would* be something you'd do. Anyway, my word is law, so you're going to prison. We'll come back for you after we've been to the palace to recover our gold and attend the banquet.'

'But—what about my graham crackers?' Killer knew she mustn't cry.

'You can have them later—if you do everything you're supposed to.'

'OK.'

Now they were carrying out the dolls to be the Duke's courtiers. Dolls and dolls—Celeste's dolls. Peachey's dolls, vacationing at Celeste's to visit their friends and relations. Killer didn't really like dolls, not even Dorothy, the most beautiful, with her long brown hair and bridal gown. She played with them, but they were not her friends. She preferred real things like babies and kittens and beach balls and toads and desserts.

Under Cissy's direction the Pretend went off perfectly. The arrival of the prince and his brothers was very exciting. With their invisible help, Elvira was tied and gagged and dragged off to prison. To make sure she would never again be free to plot against them, the three sisters and the three brothers placed pieces of cardboard (they had not told Killer this part) over the front and back entrances of the snow fort. These they covered with packed snow over which they dribbled a little boiling water. It froze almost immediately, making a nice smooth surface. Then they went off to the palace.

Of course they were not going to the palace. They were going to eat graham crackers with marshmallow and watch cartoons. They were going to tell Auntie Lil that Killer had run off to play with some children and didn't want her snack. They would be warm and giggling and eating her graham crackers. Afterwards they might take their sleds to McLin's field and have a snowball fight with the Dewhurst boys or go with them to the housing project and tip over the garbage cans.

Killer was cold and lonely. Her wet snow suit was no longer made warm by the heat of her body. They had tied her so tightly that she could not move. She looked round at her small prison of white. She could see, feel, hear the white, the whiteness of crazy nothing that scared her so much. She longed for Celeste and Cissy and Peachey. She wanted them to come and get her. She would play any game they liked, be any terrible person, she was so lonely here in the white.

They had walled her up with her accomplices in the plot—the three least loved of Celeste's dolls. They were no help. They had bad characters and did not care what became of her. Buster was a villain like she was—always trying to wreck plans, to spoil balls and ceremonies, to kidnap Dorothy. And June. June would do anything to attract men's attention. She was spiteful with short hair and told lies. She was also stupid and got the lowest marks at school. No one would ever marry June. Jackie, the dirty yellow and white rabbit, had been good at first when he arrived four years ago as an Easter Bunny. But he had allowed himself to be corrupted by Buster. Celeste said Jackie was a failure. His many crimes had made him unhappy, but it was too late for him to change his ways. Killer knew that she and Jackie and June and Buster were what Peachey's mother called Lost Souls.

Killer rubbed her tongue over her cold sore. It tasted like metal and tomatoes. She could never let it alone. Tomatoes made her think of last summer: picnics at Lake Acushnet, then fights in the car, after which she would cringe under the glare of Cissy's green eyes; Cissy and Peachey throwing jelly doughnuts at her and her throwing them back—the only time she had ever defended herself; Celeste covering her face with Ipana toothpaste in the middle of the night; Cissy and Celeste frightening her with ghost stories and tales of torture so that she lay quaking in the dark as she was quaking now in the white; Quaker Meetings on the lawn ('Quaker Meeting has begun, no more laughing, no more fun, if you show your teeth or tongue, you will have to pay a forfeit'); the Mermaid game on the beach and Cissy whipping her with one of those long flat strips of seaweed. 'Peachey, you may take one giant step. Killer, you may take one baby step.' Oh the games, the endless games she could not resist. She must always play, never say no, never complain, please them by letting them hate her and be afraid of her. It was such a funny thing. Why was it like that? She couldn't really understand Pretend. And Pretend was so important. Pretend was everything, because without it you were only yourself.

How come Cissy and Celeste could make things up? They could think so fast. If she could think fast too, she almost realized before her thoughts slid back into simply people and things and events, she might not have to be always The Crazy Doctor. Not only could Cissy and Peachey and Celeste think faster and eat faster and run faster; they seemed to need less sleep, less food, less love than she did. They seemed, with the exception of jelly doughnuts, not even to *want* any of those things. Killer longed for them. She longed for them now. But if she tried to get out of the snow fort before supper, they'd be sure to call her a spoilsport and to torment her all night long.

Better stay here a little longer and freeze. They would have to come back for her, because sooner or later they would need her for the games. They would not be able to have any of the good ones without her. She tried to feel very certain that they would come, but her heart was tightening, tightening and sinking. Her crime had been so terrible this time. No one could forgive her. Perhaps not even God could forgive her. She had broken the third commandment. She had killed the Duchess and tried to steal the inheritance. No, there was no chance of God forgiving her. He was going to let her freeze to death with Jackie and June and Buster, the Lost Souls. He would make the others forget her. He would make Auntie Lil and Uncle Raymond forget her, even her own mother and father probably. He *could* make everyone forget her. That kind of thing was easy for him. They probably had forgotten already. Or maybe it wasn't God at all. Maybe *they* wanted her to die, to freeze to death with Buster and June and Jackie. Get rid of the trouble-makers, the wicked ones, all at once. What about Mummy? She was always so kind, but that might be a Pretend too. She might really have been plotting with Cissy and the rest of them all along to wall up her little girl in a snow fort. Killer couldn't help it, she cried.

She cried until she had no more strength to cry. She began to give up, to fall asleep, to float away to a place where there was no more cold, where nothing was white, but all nice greens and reds and blues. Something was carrying her up to the sky, like Ragged Robin in the orange tree—up and up, away from the white. It was Uncle Raymond. He was pulling her out of the snow fort, he was untying her, he was picking her up in his arms, taking her to the house, muttering over her.

'Oh my God, poor Killer.' She could not open her

eyes, she was so tired. 'My God, poor little Killer.' She liked Uncle Raymond. He was a nice man.

The hospital where Killer spent the next two weeks was very white. When she first awoke, she was frightened and thought that the snow fort had grown larger and cleaner and more occupied. It was warm in the hospital (she saw quite quickly that it *was* a hospital) and there were lots of people, mainly kind, who leaned over her, gave her things, asked her questions in quiet tones, took things away, moved her about—sometimes hurting her, though not meaning to—and gazed at her for long stretches of time through her plastic tent. Their expressions were of worry, sorrow or silly cheerfulness, if grown-ups, and of questioning uncomfortableness, if children.

Killer hardly spoke. She *could* speak, she knew that, but she did not want to. She looked back through her plastic tent at all those queer expressions. Sometimes she smiled at them a little. Mostly she slept. Slept and dreamt. She dreamed they played the Mermaid game, and that she chased Cissy and Celeste and Peachey forever along an empty beach.

When she was very much better, they took the plastic tent away and let the children come near her. Cissy's green eyes were still defiant, but she spoke nicely to her sister and called her Charlotte. Killer understood that Cissy and Celeste had had some kind of punishment, but that now everyone was pretending that nothing had ever really happened.

Peachey held her hand and leaned over her. 'Bests,' Peachey whispered. Killer blinked at her. Did she mean it, was she making believe? Killer didn't understand, but smiled to let Peachey know that she was pretending she did.

Celeste even offered her Dorothy to keep forever

and be her very own. Dorothy with her bridal gown and long brown hair.

Killer hesitated. Then she spoke for the first time since the day in the snow fort.

'Can I have June instead?' she asked.

Bad Company

by Rebecca Barry

This article, reprinted from a 1995 issue of Seventeen, *advises teenage girls what to do if they find themselves in a group run by a vicious leader.*

This year you're actually *glad* to be heading back to school, and it's *not* because you're psyched to spend hours staring through a microscope and carefully sketching amoebas. You met this amazing group of girls while working at the community pool this summer, and now you're practically guaranteed a new and improved social life.

Okay, so *last* year you swore you would never be friends with these girls because they seemed so snotty, and you heard about the mean trick they once played on some girl. But it turns out that they're really sweet once you get to know them. And, of course, they're popular. And they know *hot* guys. Anyway, when you think about it, playing a trick on someone isn't *that* bad—or at least, they would never do that to you, would they?

Pam, who's in her early 20s, thinks they might. She remembers like it was yesterday the time her "friends" turned on her. "It was in the ninth grade," she says flatly. "I'll never forget it. There were seven of us, and we were basically inseparable. One day when we were walking into the cafeteria, Molly*, the leader, said, 'Hey, Diane*, come here, I have to talk to you,' and

---

* Names have been changed.

paired off with her. Then another girl said, 'Amy*, I have something to tell you,' and they split. Then the last two walked off whispering together, and I was all by myself." They never spoke to Pam again.

"I was so shocked and confused," she continues. "The way they did it, I knew it was planned, but I had no idea *why* they turned on me."

Even if you've never been on the receiving end of this kind of cattiness, chances are you've seen it happen. Maybe your group became a refuge for a girl who was dropped by another. Or maybe you saw a girl abruptly kicked out of your own crowd. Or maybe you just noticed a girl eating lunch alone and knew something had happened.

Whether this could happen to you depends on your group—who they are and what happens when they get together. Of course you're in *some* kind of group. Being part of one is as natural as borrowing your sister's clothes. You're not about to go through life without friends who still like you even after they've listened to you obsess for days about your latest trauma(s). Friends who automatically side with you no matter what—like when your parents unreasonably demand that you babysit your kid sister the night of the party your latest crush object is supposed to crash.

It's also only natural that every group be somewhat exclusive. It's not like you're *opposed* to meeting new people; it's just that maybe you're all into punk, or tennis, or Birkenstocks, or *whatever,* and other people don't seem to share your enthusiasm. Or maybe you've just known one another since you all were less than two feet tall, so other people simply assume you're a unit.

Some groups, though, are *deliberately* exclusive—and, like Pam's, not above dumping you in a heartbeat. Fortunately, these nasty groups share a few traits that can help you distinguish them from a potential circle of genuine friends.

The most obvious sign of a vicious group is a malicious leader. She might have her nice moments, but there's a side to her that really gets off on humiliating other girls. "There's this girl in my group, Shauna*, who likes to start fights," says Sondra*, 15, from Providence, Rhode Island. "When I first got in, she called me into the locker room and asked me what I thought of Nicole*, this other girl in the group. I said I thought she was a snob, because she seemed like one. Of course, Nicole was hiding nearby, listening to every word. I know Shauna set me up, but she's kind of our leader, so I didn't say anything."

In a destructive group, instead of being annoyed, the rest of the girls are usually impressed by the leader's unapologetic rudeness and go along with whatever she does.

"I think people admire the girl in my group who is the least emotional," says Jennifer*, 15, from Durand, Wisconsin. "Like she can be mean and still have lots of friends."

But these friendships are kind of twisted. Often the other girls don't actually *like* the ringleader—they're just intrigued by the challenge of her friendship. As Alicia, 16, from New York City, puts it, "When you kind of scoff, like when someone says she saw a cool movie or something and you go, 'That's great, like I care,' you become not necessarily more liked, but more *wanted*."

There's something about hypercritical people that can make you feel as if getting them to like you (or even to acknowledge your existence) is a personal achievement. It's kind of like being infatuated with a jerky guy. You become so obsessed with proving that you can have him, you conveniently forget who he really is, or that he's actually, um, a jerk.

Of course, being in this girl's circle clearly has its advantages. When she's nice to you, she's a blast, and because she's so brazen and popular, just being in her presence can make you feel pretty cool. You also get the power and prestige of being associated with someone who dominates everyone else. And in a social world where one out-of-control rumor can ruin your whole reputation, this can make life seem a little safer.

Whether you actually *are* any safer is another question, because you never know when she'll turn her mean streak on you. So you try to stay on her good side. For example, if she says another girl in the group is a flirt, you might say, "Oh, my God, did you see her at that party? She was all over *every* guy." Of course, *somehow* that girl finds out what you said—so naturally you tell her she heard wrong. And since everyone else is trying to stay in the Queen Bee's good graces, before long you all feel insecure. As Jennifer admits, "To be honest, I can't wait to get out of here and find people who don't talk behind my back."

Another sign of a vicious group is that the girls in it always laugh *at* other people instead of *with* them. Sometimes it's subtle, like they'll make a flip comment and act like they're just kidding.

"You know what I hate?" asks Lisa*, 14, from Fairfax, Virginia. "Some people in a clique will act all innocent and say, 'Your hair looks so bad today. Oh, no offense or anything'—as if they didn't mean it. Am I supposed to say, 'Thanks, I actually *like* having crusty, knotty hair?!'"

And sometimes they're more obviously cruel. When Sandra, 17, of Philadelphia, started listening to heavy metal, some girls in her class started calling her "Satan Worshiper."

"They had a slumber party, and me and a couple other class 'weirdos' were the only people who weren't invited. They videotaped the party and were making fun of us in the video, jumping around going 'I'm a freak! I'm a metalhead!' We saw it because there's this VCR in the cafeteria, and they played it at lunchtime in front of everyone."

It's possible that no one *meant* any harm—when you're in the group playing these tricks, they seem hilarious. They're also exciting, because you're all in on them together, and it feels as if nothing can stop you.

"It's like together you can break all the rules," says Joanna, 18, from New York City. "You don't really mean to be cruel. It's more like it's fun being bad."

You don't think about, or care, whether anyone on the outside thinks you're funny. Or if you do, you don't say anything, which is why it's so easy to go too far. . . .

And there's always the danger that the joke might be on you. "The worst tricks we ever played were actually on each other," says Joanna. "Once, I was supposed to meet all my friends at this coffee shop, and they just never showed up. Finally, after I'd been there for an hour by myself, they called the café. When I picked up, they were all on different extensions at someone's apartment. They were like, 'Is your refrigerator running? You better go get it.' Then they all laughed and hung up on me. I think it was because I'd had a makeover for this local magazine. It was like a way to keep me humble."

It's easy to forget that "breaking the rules" does not mean "there are no rules." Ironically, as wild as these groups might seem on the outside, there's usually an unwritten—but strict—code of behavior you're expected to follow once you're "in."

"I kind of want to stay in my clique because we are really popular," says Erin, 14, from Monterey, California. "The only problem is if you aren't an exact clone of the people in the group, you are not a part of it. . . ."

Not being yourself sometimes simply entails mild fibs, like maybe you're a closet Deadhead, but since your group is composed of Green Day fanatics, you swear you would *die* without Billie Joe. Or maybe when you're all out for pizza, you eat pepperoni even though you're a vegetarian, because you don't want to be called a "granola."

Of course, everyone does stuff like that once in a while, but in a destructive group, you might betray yourself in more serious ways. . . .

"All my friends quit playing musical instruments in, like, seventh grade," says Emily*, 18, from Cranford, New Jersey. "I really liked playing the flute—I was even taking private lessons. But I quit because my friends said it was for losers. I don't even hang out with them anymore, and I kind of wish I'd stuck with playing."

What's maddening is that after you've done all these things that made you uncomfortable, it usually turns out that no one *really* wanted to do them in the first place. "I never liked smoking," says Kendra. "I don't think any of us did. . . . Now I'm still trying to stop."

Perhaps it's because no one is allowed to truly express herself that these groups tend to define themselves by superficial things. After all, if you can't relate to one another based on how you *really* feel, or who you *really* are, you mainly share certain *things*. Like cool cars, the right look, or late curfews. Often these are things that other people don't have, or can't get, so the group gains social status by being exclusive.

"Basically, one clique in each grade rules the school," says Susan*, 15, from Bloomington, Indiana. "I'm in one of those cliques. I hate to say it's true, but we wouldn't like it if someone didn't dress well or have a good name."

They're often considered popular not because they've earned everyone's respect and approval, but because their exclusiveness perpetuates this myth that they have what everyone else wants, and are therefore having the most fun.

"In my school there's this girl, Laura, whose parents are never home. It's this big deal to be invited to her house," says Brenda*, 16, from New York City. "She knows she has power, so she's really fickle, like one week you're invited, and the next you aren't. I go there a lot. Sometimes it's pretty fun. We can smoke and have guys over. But sometimes we just sit around watching TV. It's really not *that* big of a deal."

The big secret is that the stuff they do isn't so different from everyone else. They chill with their friends, they check out new movies, they drive around looking for stuff to do, they have bad dates, and they party.

"When you're a freshman, you see these other girls dating older guys and going to senior parties, and you're like, They're so cool, how do they do that?" Amy, 17, from Scarsdale, New York, says. "But by the time you're a senior, it's like everyone starts going to all of the same parties. And then you realize that these people weren't so special—you could have done it, too." Or you might find that what made you so "uncool" is hypercool later on. When Stacey, 17, from Dallas, changed her look from classic J. Crew to alternachic, her group turned on her. "When I stopped being preppy, they made fun of me so hard," Stacey says. "They would call me a poseur and be like, 'Oh, nice hair!' Of course, they're all 'alternative' now."

If you're in a vicious clique, you *can* minimize your potential to get burned. It's possible not to participate in the stuff that makes you uncomfortable—the trick is to avoid lecturing or criticizing, or your group could get defensive and turn on you. For example, if your friends are planning to egg your biology teacher's car because she flunked someone's boyfriend, and you can't find the courage to tell them how stupid they are, just say you'd rather not take part in the yolkfest. Then make a point of not being around when it happens.

You could also widen your circle of friends by making an effort to get to know people outside of the group. Strangely enough, as seductive and fabulous as exclusive groups might seem, the people who get the most out of life are often the ones who don't limit their friends to one little circle.

"I'm glad I never got involved in being in one perfect group," says Sandra, the one who was branded a Satan worshiper. "It helped me stay focused on my work and my grades and keep friendships that last. In a clique you learn to push other people out and think that they're bad because they aren't exactly like you. It warps your perspective. You learn to value people for things that don't really matter—like what they look like or what they have."

In the end you may have more to show for it. Just ask Pam. "It was an awful experience, but it did make me a lot stronger. I learned to count on myself first, instead of depending on other people to make me feel good."

Recently Pam ran into Diane, one of the girls who'd ditched her in the cafeteria that day. When Pam asked why they did it, Diane shrugged and said, "Oh, we thought you were gay."

"What-*ever*," laughs Pam, who is straight, but whose diverse group of friends includes both gay and straight people. "At least I know it had more to do with them than me."